Christian Crusaders

Songs and Solos Used by the Christian Crusaders in their

Special Soul-Saving Work

Adapted for the Church, Grove, School, Choir and Home

Christian Crusaders

Songs and Solos Used by the Christian Crusaders in their Special Soul-Saving Work
Adapted for the Church, Grove, School, Choir and Home

ISBN/EAN: 9783337296384

Printed in Europe, USA, Canada, Australia, Japan

Cover: Foto ©Thomas Meinert / pixelio.de

More available books at **www.hansebooks.com**

HEAVEN FOR THE RIGHTEOUS AND
HELL FOR THE WICKED.

Songs and Solos

USED BY THE

Christian Crusaders

IN THEIR SPECIAL SOUL-SAVING WORK,

AND ADAPTED FOR THE

CHURCH, GROVE, SCHOOL, CHOIR, AND HOME.

HEADQUARTERS,

98 FRONT ST., WORCESTER, MASS.

P. O. Box 469.

THERE IS NO HOPE

Of any being saved who do not see that they are in danger of hell and that they must give up sin and follow Christ to escape.

Of any being happy till they are certain God has pardoned their sins.

Of any saving souls till they see that it is their work, and that God will help them to do it.

Of any being good soldiers till they are willing to die to save the world.

Of any conquering till they see they are helpless, but that God means them always to triumph.

Of any one having a good eternity in heaven, who did not make a good fight for God on earth.

WANTED

MEN AND WOMEN

Who are certain that God has saved them from their sins and that they are ready to die.

Who are not "too wide-awake" to believe like little children all that God says in His book.

Who believe that they have deserved to go to hell.

Who are not afraid to stand on their own doorsteps, or in their workshop, to tell all they know about Jesus.

Who value leisure from every day work chiefly for the opportunity it gives them to save souls.

Who believe God not only expects them to save their own souls, but to save others as well.

Who really spend all the time and strength they can already in doing so, and who only wish to go forth in the Lord's name to spend more strength and time for him.

Who would really spend the time not occupied with public services in visiting from door to door.

Who would not stop any meeting, or cease from any sort of work, because the clock had reached some particular point, but would persevere until victory was won, no matter at what cost of time or strength.

Who wished to be offered up to save other people.

APPLY TO

HEADQUARTERS,

P. O. Box 469. - - - - - - Worcester, Mass.

Walking in the Light.

Changed by E. L. K.

1. { Of Him who did salvation bring, We're walking in the beautiful light of God.
   { With all my heart I love to sing, We're walking in the beautiful light of . .

2. { Ask but His grace, and lo! 't is giv'n; We're walking in the beautiful light of God.
   { Ask, and He turns your hell to heav'n, We're walking in the beautiful light of . .

CHORUS.

God, } We are walk - - ing in the light, We are

in the light, in the light,

walk - - ing in the light, We are walk - - ing in the

in the light, in the light, in the light,

light, We are walk-ing in the beautiful light of God.

in the light.

3 Though sin and sorrow hurt my soul,
Jesus, Thy balm has made me whole.

4 Let all the world come here and know
What saving love our God will show.

5 All day long to this spring I fly;
I drink, and yet am ever dry.

3

2. I've Anchored my Soul.

Arr. by E. L. K.

1. I am rest-ing so sweet-ly in Je - sus now! I
2. Oh, long on the o - cean my bark was toss'd, Where
3. Oh, how sweet in the ha - ven of rest to hide, No

Cho. *I have an-chored my soul in the ha-ven of rest,* I

sail the wide sea no more; The tempest may sweep o'er the
tem-pests and storms ne'er cease! My heart was in fear, and no
bil - lows of doubt or fear! The o - cean may roll, but there's

sail the wide seas no more; The tempests may sweep o'er the

wild, storm-y deep, I'm safe where the storms come no more.
ref - uge was near, Till in Je - sus my soul found her peace.
rest for the soul When the voice of my Sav - iour is near.

wild, storm - y deep, But in Je - sus I'm safe ev - er - more.

3. I'll Have a Full Salvation.

1 I'll have a full salvation,
From sinful ways retire,
Give up myself to Jesus,
Be filled with holy fire;
Doubting and fear bring trouble,
Conscience will never rest,
Until I have the witness,
Love burning in my breast.

CHORUS.
I'll have a full salvation, saved from
the power of sin;
Washed in the blood of Jesus, whiter
than snow within. ·

2 I'll have a full salvation,
And leave the world behind,

Be saved from sinful tempters,
Saved from the carnal mind;
Parting with every idol,
I will myself disown,
Lay all upon the altar,
And be the Lord's alone.

3 I'll have a full salvation,
In holiness to walk;
In private and in public
Will with the Master talk;
To keep me every moment
Salvation has been given;
I'll have a full salvation,
Heaven all the way to heaven.

4

4 We'll Arise and Shine.

Arr. by E. L. K.

1. See Dan-iel in the den of roar-ing li-ons, See Dan-
2. And so the li-ons could not him de-vour, And
3. See the He-brew chil-dren in the fier-y fur-nace,See the
4. For Je-sus saved them by His might-y pow-er, For Je-
5. See Paul and Si-las bound with-in the dun-geon,See Paul
6. See Pe-ter chained and ly-ing in the dun-geon, See Pe-

Cho. We'll a - rise and shine, give God the glo - ry, We'll

iel in the den of roar-ing li-ons,But the an-gel stood be-
so the li-ons could not him de-vour,For Je-sus saved him by
He-brew children in the fiery furnace,Oh,the flam-ing fire up-
us saved them by His might-y pow-er,And they walked to-geth-er
and Si-las bound with-in the dungeon,Oh,the pris-on doors were
ter chained and ly-ing in the dungeon,Oh,the an-gel burst the

a - rise and shine,give God the glo-ry, We'll a - rise and shine,

fore the roar-ing lions, In the year of Ju - bi - lee.
His might-y pow-er In the year of Ju - bi - lee.
on them had no pow'r. In the year of Ju - bi - lee.
in the flam-ing fire, In the year of Ju - bi - lee.
o - pened by the pow'r In the year of Ju - bi - lee.
gate and chain asunder, In the year of Ju - bi - lee.

give God the glo - ry, In the year of Ju - bi - lee.

5 Oh, the Blood.

1 It is the blood that washes white,
That makes me pure within,
That keeps the inward witness right
That cleanses from all sin.

CHORUS.

Oh, the blood to me so dear,
Saving now from guilt and fear,
Cleansing now my heart within,
Making free from self and sin.

2 It is the blood that sweeps away
The power of Satan's rod,
That shows the new and living way
That leads to heaven and God.

3 It is the blood that open'd wide
God's full salvation gate;
The blood that turned the veil aside
To show the Holiest state.

4 It is the blood that brings us nigh
To Holiness and heaven,
The source of victory and joy;
God's life for rebels given.

Marching on.

Words and music by CAPT. JOHNSON.

1. Marching on   in the light of God, Marching on,   I   am marching on;
2. Marching on thro' the hosts of sin, Marching on,   I   am marching on;
3. Marching on while the skep-tics sneer, Marching on,   I   am marching on;
4. Marching on with the flag unfurled, Marching on,   I   am marching on;
5. Marching on with the "Blood and Fire," Marching on, I   am marching on;

CHORUS.

Up the path that the Master trod, Marching, marching   on.   A robe of white, a
Victory's mine while I've Christ within, Marching, marching   on.
Per-fect love casteth out all fear.   Marching, marching   on.
Preaching Christ to the dying world, Marching, marching   on.
On till the Lord shall say, "Come up higher." Marching, marching on.

crown of gold, A harp, a home, a mansion fair, A   victor's palm, a

joy un-told, Are mine when I get there. For Je-sus is my Saviour, He's

wash'd my sins away, Paid my debt on Calv'ry's mountain, Happy in His dying love,

Marching on. Concluded.

Sing-ing all the day, I'm liv - ing, yes, I'm liv-ing in the Foun-tain.

7 Oh, it is Glory!

Joyful.

1. I'm a sol - dier bound for glo - ry, March - ing
Cho.—*Oh, it is glo - ry! oh, it is glo - ry! Oh, it is*

at my King's command; Let me tell my pleasing
glo - ry in my soul, For I have touch'd the hem of His

D.C.

sto - ry, As we march to Ca - naan's land.
gar - ment, And His blood doth make me whole.

2 I was once so sad and weary —
  Weary of my load of sin,
Till I cried " Lord Jesus save me,"
And He smiled and took me in.
  Oh, it is glory, etc.

3 Now my life is constant pleasure,
  Jesus is my bosom friend,
He is such a precious treasure
That my joys can never end.
  Oh, it is glory, etc.

4 Jesus loves me, Jesus saves me,
  Jesus is my sweetest song;
Jesus altogether lovely,
Jesus, Jesus, all along.
  Oh, it is glory, etc.

5 I shall meet Him in the glory,
  I shall see Him face to face :
He will take me to my mansion,
Where he has prepared a place.
  Oh, it is glory, etc.

6 Then upon the golden pavement,
  Robed in glory I shall stand,
Praising Him who died to save me :
Glory, glory to the Lamb.
  Oh, it is glory, etc.

Marching to Glory.

W. F. SHERWIN. Ch'd by H. T. C.   H. C. WORK. Arr. by H. T. C.

1. Come with hearts and voi-ces now and sing a gos-pel song,
2. Gird the gos-pel ar-mor on and du-ty's call o-bey;
3. For-ward then to bat-tle 'neath the ban-ner of the cross;
4. We shall win the vic-t'ry by the pow-er of the Word:

Sing it with a spir-it that will move the might-y throng;
See the host of Sa-tan read-y mar-shalled for the fray;
Count-ing world-ly hon-ors at their best as on-ly dross;
This our glo-rious wea-pon, 'tis the Spir-it's might-y sword,

S.

Sing it till the world shall hear the ech-oes loud and long,
Go-ing forth to meet them we will watch and fight and pray,
Je-sus is our Cap-tain, and we ne'er can suf-fer loss,
We shall sure-ly con-quer, 'tis the prom-ise of the Lord,

D. S. *Now we'll shout sal-va-tion o-ver moun-tain, land, and sea,*

FINE. CHORUS.

While we are march-ing to glo-ry! Then hail! all hail the
While we are march-ing to glo-ry!
While we are march-ing to glo-ry!
For we are march-ing to glo-ry!

While we are march-ing to glo-ry!

D.S.

com-ing ju-bi-lee! Re-deemed from sin, our Jesus makes us free;

I Believe Jesus Saves.

1. Let us sing of His love once again; Of the love that can nev-er de-
2. There are cleansing and healing for all Who will wash in the life-giv-ing
3. Ev-en now, while we taste of His love, We are filled with delight at His

cay, Of the blood of the Lamb who was slain, Till we
flood; There is life ev-er-last-ing and joy At the
name; Oh, what will it be, when a-bove We shall

CHORUS.

praise Him a-gain in that day. I be-lieve Je-sus
right hand of God, thro' His blood.
join in the song of the Lamb.

I be-lieve

saves, And His blood makes me whiter than snow, I be-

Je-sus saves, than snow,

lieve Je-sus saves, And His blood makes me whiter than snow.

I be-lieve Je-sus saves,

4 Then we'll march in His name till we come
At His bidding to enter our rest;
And the Father shall welcome us home [blest.
To our place in the realms of the

5 So with banners unfurled to the breeze,
Our motto shall "Holiness" be,
Till the crown from His hand we shall seize,
And the King in His glory we see.

1. How bold and brave the right-eous are; From fear and sin set
2. With ho-ly bold-ness we will fight, Our Cap-tain leads us
3. We'll strive to spread thro' all the world The news of God's free

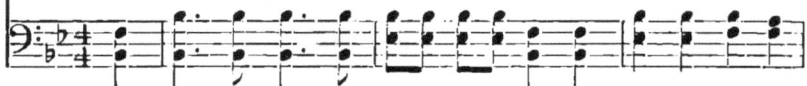

free, They dare to fight, like men of war, For right and lib-er-ty.
on Op-pos-ing wrong, uphold-ing right, Grand vic'tries shall be won.
grace, Re-demp-tion's sto-ry shall be told, To all the fallen race.

CHORUS.

We'll lift up the banner on high, The Salvation banner of love, We'll

fight be-neath its colors till we die, Then march to our home a-bove.

4 We'll fight like loyal warriors here,
And when the battle's o'er,
Our crown of glory we shall wear
On heaven's eternal shore.

5 The battle will be fierce and long;
But when the end shall come,
Then we will sing the victor's song,
In our eternal Home.

And as Moses lifted up the serpent in the wilderness, even so must the Son of Man be lifted up; that whosoever believeth on him should not perish but have eternal life. Jno. 3: 14, 15.

And I, if I be lifted up from the earth, will draw all men unto me. Jno. 12: 32.

Rally Round the Banner.

W. F. S.

W. F. S.

1. Sound the battle cry! See! the foe is nigh; Raise the standard high, For the Lord;
2. Strong to meet the foe, Marching on we go, While our cause we know, Must prevail;
3. Oh! Thou God of all, Hear us when we call, Help us one and all   By Thy grace;

Gird your arm-or on. Stand firm ev-'ry one; Rest your cause upon His ho-ly word.
Shield and banner bright, Gleaming in the light; Battling for the right, We ne'er shall fail.
When the battle's done, And the vict'ry won, May we wear the crown, Before Thy face.

CHORUS.

Rouse, then, sol - diers, ral - ly round the ban-ner, Read - y, stead - y,

pass   the word   a - long;   On - ward,   for - ward

shout a - loud Ho -san-na! Christ is cap -tain of the might -y throng.

Happy in the Lord.

1. { A pil-grim and a stran-ger here, Hap-py, hap-py,
   { Dear friends have reached that bliss-ful shore, Hap-py, hap-py,

2. { I leave this world of sin be-hind, Hap-py, hap-py,
   { Fair lands are here, and hous-es fair, Hap-py, hap-py,

hap - py, I seek the home to pil-grims dear, Hap-py in the Lord.
hap - py, They sor-row not and sigh no more, Hap-py in the Lord.

hap - py, That bet-ter home in heav'n to find, Hap-py in the Lord.
hap - py, But fair-er is my home up there, Hap-py in the Lord.

CHORUS.

We'll cross the riv - er of Jor - dan, Hap - py, hap - py,

hap - py, hap-py, Cross the riv-er of Jor - dan, Hap -py in the Lord.

3 O happy day when first Thy love,
    Happy, happy, happy,
  Began our grateful hearts to move,
    Happy in the Lord,
  And gazing on Thy wondrous cross
    Happy, happy, happy,
  We saw all else as worthless dross,
    Happy in the Lord.

4 O happy day! when we shall see,
    Happy, happy, happy,
  And fix our longing eyes on Thee,
    Happy in the Lord,   [Love,
  On Thee, our Light, our Life, our
    Happy, happy, happy,
  Our All below, our Heaven above,
    Happy in the Lord.

I Am a Child of a King.

Not too fast.

1. I'm a christian sol - dier—Of the tried and faithful few;
2. They sing and shout in heav - en—It is their hearts' de - light;
3. My sins are all for - giv - en, Which did as moun-tains rise;

Cho. *I am a child of a King. I am, I am a child of a King,*

I shout when I am hap - py, And that I mean to do.
I'll shout when I am hap - py, And that with all my might.
My ti - tle 's clear for heav - en—Yon coun-try in the skies.

It is, it is a glorious thing To be a child of a King.

Some say I am too noi - sy, I know the rea - son why;
I've Je - sus Christ with - in me—He 's turned the dev - il out;
God's saints are my com - pan-ions; I'm bound for end - less day;

I am a child of a King. I am, I am a child of a King,

And if they felt the glo - ry They'd shout as well as I.
And when I feel the glo - ry It makes me sing and shout.
And tho' the storms are rag - ing, I'll sail a - long the way.

It is, it is a glorious thing, To be a child of a King.

1. O'er Co-lum-bia, from ocean to o - cean, The Christian Crusaders you'll
2. We see how sin's des-o - la - tion, Now threatens our land to de-
3. The out-cast, the drunkard bring hither, And all steeped in sin to the

see; Filled with love and a Sav - iour's de - vo - tion, Ev - 'ry-
form, On Christ, our "Rock and Foun-da - tion," There's
brim, May zeal for our Mas - ter ne'er with - er, Nor de-

where slaves of sin set-ting free; Our meet-ings make ma -ny as-
safe - ty a - lone from the storm; With the blood-stained ban-ner
sire for His glo - ry grow dim; May we from His ser - vice ne'er

sem - ble, "Je - sus on - ly," we lift up to view; And we'll
o'er us, Though on - ly a tried faith -ful few, In the
sev - er, But ev - er to Je - sus prove true, And

shout un -til Sa - tan doth tremble, Sinners, there is sal-va-tion for you.
name of our captain we'll conquer, And tell sinners, there's salvation for you.
this be our war-cry for-ev -er. Sinners, there is sal-va-tion for you.

Salvation for You. Concluded.

CHORUS.

Oh, yes, there's salvation for you, Oh, yes, there's salva-tion for you, For

you on the cross Je-sus suf-fered, Oh, yes, there's salvation for you.

15 Salvation in the Heart.

Arr. by E. L. K. and W. P.

1. I'm glad I've got sal - va-tion In my heart,   I'm
2. I want to be like Je -sus, In my heart,   I
3. I will not be de -ceit-ful In my heart,   I
4. I want to love my neighbor, In my heart,   I

In my heart,

glad I've got sal -vation In my heart,   In my heart,   In my
want to be like Je-sus, In my heart,   In my heart,   In my
will not be de-ceit-ful, In my heart,   In my heart,   In my
want to love my neighbor, In my heart,   In my heart,   In my

in my heart,

heart,   I'm glad I've got sal-va-tion   In my heart.
heart,   I want to be like Je-sus,   In my heart.
heart,   I will not be de -ceit-ful   In my heart.
heart,   I want to love my neighbor, In my heart.

In my heart,

5 I want to love my enemies,   6 I feel the spirit burning,
  In my heart, etc.   15   In my heart, etc.

16 Brightly Gleams our Banner.

T. J. POTTER. Arr.   ARTHUR SULLIVAN.

1. Brightly gleams our ban - ner, Point-ing to the sky, Waving wand'rers
2.   Je -sus, Lord and Mas - ter, At Thy sa-cred feet, Here, with hearts re-
3.   All our days di - rect us In the way to go, Lead us on vic-
4.   Then with saints and an - gels May we join a - bove, Offering prayers and

on - ward   To their home on   high; Journeying o'er a   des - ert,
joic - ing,   See Thy children   meet; Oft -en have we   left   Thee,
to - rious,   O - ver ev - 'ry   foe, Bid Thine an-gel   shield   us,
prais - es   At Thy throne of   love; When the toil is   o - ver

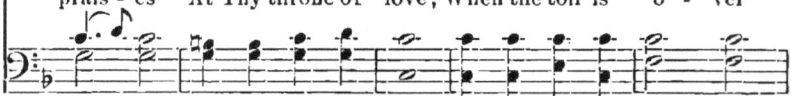

Glad-ly thus we   pray, And with hearts u-nit - ed,   Take our heav'nward way.
Oft-en gone a -stray, Keep us, mighty Sav - iour,   In the narrow way.
When the storm clouds lower, Be our great de -liv - 'rer,   In the dy-ing hour.
Then come rest and peace, Jesus in His beau - ty,   Songs that never cease.

CHORUS.

Bright -ly gleams our   ban -   ner,   Point -ing to   the

sky,   Wav-ing wand'rers   on - ward   To their home on   high.
sky, Wav -ing   wan -   d'rers

16

17 Blessed Assurance.

Words by FANNIE CROSBY. Music by Mrs. Jos. F. KNAPP.

1. Bless-ed as - sur-ance, Je -sus is mine! Oh, what a fore-taste of
2. Per-fect sub-mis-sion, per-fect de -light, Vi-sions of rap-ture burst
3. Per-fect sub-mis -sion, all is at rest, I in my Sav -iour am

glo - ry di -vine! Heir of sal-va - tion, purchased of God, Born of His
on my sight; Angels de-scending, bring from a-bove, Echoes of
hap-py and blest; Watching and waiting, looking a-bove, Fill'd with His

CHORUS.

Spir - it, wash'd in His blood. This is my sto - ry, this is my
mer - cy, whis-pers of love.
good -ness, lost in His love.

song, Praising my Sav -iour all the day long, This is my sto - ry,

this is my song, Prais-ing my Sav - iour all the day long.

18 Down Where the Living Waters Flow.

1. Once I was far in sin, But Jesus took me in,
2. With Jesus by my side, I need no other guide,
3. When fighting here is o'er, I shall rest for-ev-more,

Down where the living wa-ters flow: 'Twas there He gave me sight,
Down where the living wa-ters flow: He is my hope and stay,
Down where the living wa-ters flow: I shall join the bloodwash'd throng,

And let me see the light, Down where the living wa-ters flow.
And He saves me all the way, Down where the living wa-ters flow.
And sing the highway songs, Down where the living wa-ters flow.

CHORUS.

Down where the living wa-ters flow, Down where the tree of life doth grow, I'm

liv-ing in the light, for Jesus now I fight, Down where the living waters flow.

18

Go Forth and Reap.

Isaac Watts.

C. Strauble.

1. A - las! and did my Saviour bleed? And did, and did my Sovereign die? Would He devote that sa-cred head For such a worm as I?
2. Was it for crimes that I had done, He groaned, He groaned up-on the tree? Amazing pity! grace unknown! And love beyond degree.
3. Well might the sun in darkness hide, And shut, and shut his glories in, When Christ, the mighty Maker, died For man, the creature's sin.

CHORUS.

The Mas-ter calls, go forth and reap, The Master calls, go forth and reap; His sweet voice calls go forth and reap, go forth and reap.

4 Thus might I hide my blushing face, [Cross appears;
Whilst His, whilst His dear
Dissolve my heart in thankfulness,
And melt mine eyes to tears.

5 But drops of grief can ne'er re-pay
The debt, the debt of love I owe;
Here, Lord, I give myself away,
'T is all that I can do.

I will Follow Thee.

Arr. by E. L. K.

1. Je-sus, I my cross have taken, All to leave and follow Thee! Naked,
2. Let the world despise and leave me, They have left my Saviour too; Human
3. Man may trouble and distress me, 'Twill but drive me to Thy breast, Life with

poor, despised, for-sak - en, Thou from hence my all shall be. Perish
hearts and looks deceive me: Thou art not like them untrue; And while
tri - als hard may press me, Heaven will bring me sweeter rest. O 'tis

ev-'ry fond am - bi - tion, All I've sought, or hoped, or known; Yet how
Thou shalt smile up-on me, God of wisdom, love and might, Foes may
not in grief to harm me, While Thy love is left to me! O 'twere

rich is my con-di - tion! God and heav'n are still my own.
hate and friends may shun me, Show Thy face and all is bright.
not in joy to charm me, Were that joy unmixed with Thee.

CHORUS.

I will fol -low Thee, my Sav - iour: Thou did'st shed Thy blood for

I Will Follow Thee. Concluded.

me, And tho' all men should forsake Thee, By Thy grace I'll follow Thee.

21 The Wide, Wide World.

Arr. by E. L. K.

1. They tell me there are dangers In the path my feet must tread, But they
2. They tell me life has tri-als, And the fairest hopes will flee, But I
3. Once my heart was ver-y sin-ful, And my love for God was small, But

can - not see the glo - ry That is shin - ing round my head.
trust my all in Je - sus, And I know He cares for me.
Je - sus' blood has reach'd me, And thro' Him I con - quer all.

CHORUS.

Oh 'tis Je - sus guides my footsteps, He has made my heart His

own And I would not dare to journey Thro' this wide, wide world a-lone.

21

Tell It to Jesus.

J. E. RANKIN, D. D. Matt. 14: 12. E. S. LORNE.

1. Are you wea-ry, are you heav-y-heart-ed? Tell it to Je-sus,
2. Do the tears flow down your cheek unbidden? Tell it to Je-sus,
3. Do you fear the gath'ring clouds of sorrow? Tell it to Je-sus,
4. Are you trou-bled at the tho't of dy - ing? Tell it to Je-sus,

Tell it to Je - sus. Are you griev-ing o - ver joys de-part-ed?
Tell it to Je - sus. Have you sins that to man's eye are hid - den?
Tell it to Je - sus. Are you an-xious what shall be to-mor-row?
Tell it to Je - sus. For Christ's coming Kingdom are you sighing?

CHORUS.

Tell it to Je - sus a - lone. Tell it to Je - sus,

Tell it to Je-sus, He is a friend well known; You have no oth-er

such a friend or broth-er, Tell it to Je - sus a - lone.

I Want to be a Worker.

" The laborers are few." Matt. 9: 27.

I. B.

I. BALTZELL.

1. I want to be a worker with the Lord. I want to love and trust His holy
2. I want to be a worker ev-'ry day, I want to lead the erring in the
3. I want to be a worker strong and brave, I want to trust in Jesus' pow'r to
4. I want to be a worker; help me, Lord, To lead the lost and erring to Thy

word; I want to sing and pray, and be bus-y ev -'ry day In the
way, That leads to heav'n a-bove, where all is peace and love, In the
save; All who will tru -ly come, shall find a hap-py home In the
word, That points to joys on high, where pleasures never die, In the

Chorus.

vine-yard of the Lord. I will work, I will pray, In the
king-dom of the Lord.
king-dom of the Lord.
king-dom of the Lord. I will work and pray, I will work and pray,

vine-yard, in the vine-yard of the Lord, of the Lord, I will work, I will

pray, I will la-bor ev -'ry day In the vine-yard of the Lord.

The Lily of the Valley.

1. I've found a friend in Jesus, He's everything to me. He's the fairest of ten
2. He all my griefs has taken, and all my sorrows borne ; In temptation He's my
3. He'll nev-er, never leave me, nor yet forsake me here, While I live by faith and

thousand to my soul ; The Li-ly of the Valley in Him alone I see, All I
strong and mighty tow'r : I've all for Him forsaken ; I've all my idols torn From my
do His blessed will : A wall of fire about me, I've nothing now to fear, With His

need to cleanse and make me fully whole ; In sorrow He's my comfort, in trouble He's my
heart, and now He keeps me by His pow'r ; Tho' all the world forsake me, and Satan tempts me
manna He my hungry soul shall fill ; Then sweeping up to glory, we see His blessed

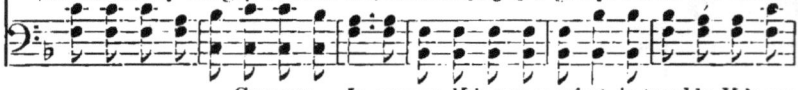

CHORUS. *In sorrow He's my comfort, in trouble He's my*

Hallelujah

stay, He tells me ev-'ry care on Him to roll, He's the Li - ly of the
sore, Thro' Je-sus I shall safely reach the goal. He's the Li - ly of the
face, Where riv-ers of delight shall ev-er roll. He's the Li - ly of the

stay, He tells me ev -'ry care on Him to roll, He's the Li - ly of the

D.S.

Val-ley, the bright and morning Star, He's the fairest of ten thousand t' my soul.

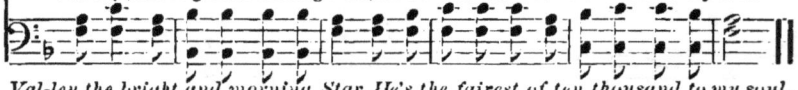

Val-ley, the bright and morning Star, He's the fairest of ten thousand to my soul.

25 The Well of Full Salvation.

John 4: 14.

1. { What joy in serving Jesus, It is our heart's delight; We praise Him for His
    { His love it is so balmy, His peace it is so sweet, Our ev'ry breath's a

2. { In heav'n we'll see our Jesus, The blessed Lamb of God, He from our sins re-
    { The world, with all its pleasures, Have sunk beneath our view, We have laid up all our

CHORUS.

good-ness, And that with all   our might. } We are drinking at the
pray - er,   In him our joy's   com-plete. }
lieves us;   He is   our staff   and rod. }
treasures   In the land be-yond   the blue. }

well of Full Sal-va - tion, Where the Sav-iour gives to all so full and

free,   And he keeps us from the pow'r of all temp-ta - tion: Won't you

come along and have a drink with me?

3 Methinks I hear the chorus,
    Every note so clear and true,
Of the hundred and forty-four
        thousand,—
    Oh, what a happy crew!
All those who love the Saviour,
    Will mingle with that throng,
And praise His name forever
    In everlasting song!

25

1. We are sweeping thro' the land, With the sword of God in hand, We are
2. Oh, the blessed Lord of light, We will serve Him with our might, And His
3. We are sweeping on to win Perfect vic-t'ry o-ver sin, And we'll

watching and we're pray-ing, while we fight; On the wings of love we'll fly, To the
arm shall bring sal-va-tion to the poor; They shall lean upon His breast, Know the
shout our Saviour's prais-es ev-er-more; When the strife on earth is done, And some

souls a-bout to die, And we'll force them to behold the precious light!
sweetness of His rest,—Of His pardon He the vilest will as-sure.
mil-lion souls we've won, We'll rejoin our conqu'ring comrades gone be-fore.

CHORUS.

Over there, over there, I shall never know a sorrow over there: In the
over there, over there, over there,

streets of shining gold, with the glory in my soul, I shall never know a sorrow over there.
o-ver there.

26

27 The Heart that Knows no Sorrow.

Words and Music by J. M. Sawers.

1. The heart that knows no sor - row is the heart that rests in
2. Trust on, keep ev - er trust - ing, the bat - tle's al - most
3. Soon, soon, our eyes shall see Him, the roy - al Prince of
4. With love and pure de - vo - tion we'll live in end - less

God, Whose peace is like a riv - er, so tran - quil, deep, and
o'er, O list to the sweet mu - sic of the harps on the golden
heaven, All robed in gor-geous splen-dor, the Rock for sin - ners
day, No heart shall know a sor - row, all tears are wiped a-

broad; A - mid the storm and tem - pest, a lov - ing hand is
shore: My soul is filled with glad - ness, my heart is all a -
riven; Our joy shall be ec - stat - ic, our peace shall know no
way: And there with all our loved ones, we'll sing the new, new

rit.

near, To guide us thro' in safe - ty, and calm our ev - 'ry fear.
glow, The angels are playing their heav'nly strains to cheer us here be - low.
end, All thro' the corridors of bliss, our prais-es they shall wend.
song, And shout our glad ho - san - nas with all the ransomed throng.

28 Everywhere.

1 Who'll fight for the Lord every-
    where,   [light,
  Till we march by the river of
  Where the Lamb leads His host free
    from care,   [white?
  All robed in their garments of
  Everywhere who'll fight for the
    Lord everywhere?

2 Oh, think of the fiends everywhere,
  Who on man's ruined nature have
    trod,
  Of the curses that breathe on the air,

From souls wandering far from
  their God.

3 Oh, Saviour, lead me everywhere,
  Till each sin-burdened soul
    knows Thy rest,
  Till the prey from the Mighty we
    tear,   [is blest.
  And our country with Thy peace

4 I'll fight for the Lord everywhere,
  For the terrible need I can see.
  Many dying in sin everywhere,
  My Jesus alone can set free.

27

Let the Light of Jesus Come.

J. M. S.   J. M. SAWERS.

1. I have oft - en prom-ised Je - sus, That my heart would be His
2. Long my heart has known its du - ty, But re-fused to do Thy
3. Let my heart its doors throw o - pen, And in - vite my Je - sus
4. Where Thou art is joy and glad - ness, Comfort, peace, unbounding

own, But from day to day neg -lect-ed, Un - til it cold had grown.
will; Now I can hold out no long - er, Come, my hungry soul and fill.
in; There to reign su-preme, all-glo-rious, There to dwell in place of sin.
love; Fit, pre-pare me, for Thy kingdom, There t' en -joy Thy bliss above.

CHORUS.

light . . . . . of Je - sus come,   Let the

Let the light of Je-sus come, Oh, let the light of Je-sus come, With His

light . . . . . . of Je - sus come,   With His

all - a - ton - ing mer - cy, Let the light of Je - sus come, Let the

all . . . . a - ton - ing mer - cy,   Let the

light of Je - sus come Oh, let the light of Je - sus come, With His

Let the Light of Jesus Come. Concluded.

light . . . . of Je - sus come.

all - a - ton - ing, mer - cy, Let the light of Je - sus come.

30 Since I've Trusted Him.

F. A. B.   F. A. BLACKMER.

1. Once I tho't I walked with Jesus, Yet such changeful feelings had;
2. But He call'd me closer to Him, Bade my doubting, fearing, cease;
3. Now, I'm trusting ev'ry moment, Nothing less can be e - nough;

Some-times trusting, sometimes doubting, Sometimes joyful, sometimes sad.
And when I had ful -ly yield-ed, Filled my soul with perfect peace.
And the Saviour bears me gently, O'er those places once so rough.

CHORUS.

Oh, the peace the Saviour gives, Peace I never knew be-fore;

And my way has brighter grown, Since I've learned to trust Him more.

29

There's a Palm.

Words and Music by J. M. SAWERS.

Cheerful.

1. Come all ye reb-els home to God, Whom Je-sus died to
2. There's mercy for you with the Lord, If you'll but seek His
3. This lov-ing Je-sus ne'er re-pels, The soul that seeks His
4. The joy that fills our souls just now, It can-not be ex-

save; And fight beneath His lov-ing wings, And be a sol-dier brave.
face; Re-pent, believe, your vows renew, And trust Him for His grace.
love! O, try with all your ransomed powers to live for Heav'n a-bove.
press'd; But this I know, if we prove true, With Je-sus we shall rest.

CHORUS. *Quicker.*

There's a palm, there's a palm, There's a palm of vic-to-

ry, Hal-le-lu-jah! There's a palm, There's a

palm . . . There's a palm for you and me.

The Precious Blood.

J. M. SAWERS.   J. M. SAWERS.

1. Far from God and home I wandered, Grieved the God who
2. Home a-gain to Father's dwelling, Home a-gain, no
3. Nev-er more this world shall charm me, Ma-ny charms it

loved me so, But He sought un-til He found me, Saved me
more to roam, Now I mean to do His bid-ding, Nev-er
had for me, For I've found a charm far sweeter, Christ, my

CHORUS.

from all sin and woe. Oh, the precious blood, Oh the precious blood, The
more to walk a-lone.
im-mor-tal-i-ty.

blood that was shed on Cal-va-ry; Oh, the pre-cious blood,

Oh, the pre-cious blood, The blood that was shed for me.

33 Going Up.

Words by Jas. Nicholson.   Music by Asa Hull. Used by per.

1. Go-ing up, to the joys ev-er-lasting, My friends and companions to meet,
2. Go-ing up, to   unite with the voices That like "many waters" doth sound;
3. Go-ing up, with a faith calm and stead-y, My day's work completed at noon,

Where sanctified millions are casting, Their crowns at Emanuel's feet.
My soul   in the prospect rejoic - es, With glory I soon shall be crown'd.
Oh, "tell ev'ry one   to be_read-y, " The master may call for them soon.

Chorus.

Going up to my purchas'd possession, Going up, to my permanent rest;

Going up, with the ho-ly procession, Going up, at my Saviour's behest.

34 Come, Sinner, Come.

1 While Jesus whispers to you,
Come, sinner, come!
While we are praying for you,
Come, sinner, come!
Now is the time to own Him,
Come, sinner, come!
Now is the time to know Him,
Come, sinner, come!

2 Are you too heavy laden?
Come, sinner, come!

Jesus will bear your burden,
Come, sinner come!
Jesus will not deceive you,
Come, sinner, come!
Jesus can now redeem you
Come, sinner, come!

3 Oh, hear His tender pleading,
Come, sinner, come!
Come and receive the blessing,
Come, sinner, come!
While Jesus whispers to you,
Come, sinner, come!
While we are praying for you,
Come, sinner, come!

Ring those Heavenly Bells.

Capt. C. P. B.

1. Hear the Saviour's loving call, Friend, will you come to Him? Leave the sin, the
2. Do not turn your back on God, Friend, will you come to Him? 'Twas for you He
3. The way, narrow it is true, Friend, will you come to Him? There is one who'll
4. Will you cling to things on earth, Friend, will you come to Him? Oh how tri-fling

world and all, Lost one, will you come? Strive to en - ter at the gate,
shed that blood, Lost one, will you come? You will nev-er have true rest,
take you thro', Lost one, will you come? Lift the bur - den from your soul,
is their worth, Lost one, will you come? Scorn-ful frowns of those you see,

Friend, will you come? 'Tis not wise for you to wait, Lost one, will you come?
Friend, will you come? Till by Him you have been bless'd, Lost one, will you come?
Friend, will you come? Place your name on heaven's roll, Lost one, will you come?
Friend, will you come? Will not ring those bells for thee, Lost one, will you come?

CHORUS.

They are waiting up there to ring the bells to - night, Ring those bells, heavenly bells,

Ring, ring.

Ring for you when your soul gets the light, Ring those heav-en - ly bells.

Sun of My Soul.

"The Lord God is a sun." — Psalm 74: 11.

JOHN KEBLE, 1827.　　　　　　　German.　Arr. by W. H. MONK.

1. Sun of my soul, Thou Saviour dear, It is not night if Thou be near;
2. When the soft dews of kindly sleep My wearied eye-lids gen-tly steep,
3. Abide with me from morn till eve, For without Thee I can-not live;
4. If some poor wandering child of Thine Have spurned to-day the voice di-vine—

Oh, may no earth-born cloud a-rise, To hide Thee from Thy servant's eyes.
Be my last thought, how sweet to rest, For-ev-er on my Saviour's breast.
Abide with me when night is nigh, For without Thee I dare not die.
Now, Lord, the gracious work be-gin; Let him no more lie down in sin.

5 Watch by the sick; enrich the poor
　With blessings from Thy boundless
　　store;
　Be every mourner's sleep to-night,
　Like infant's slumbers, pure and
　　light.

6 Come near and bless us when we
　　wake, [take,
　Ere through the world our way we
　Till in the ocean of Thy love
　We lose ourselves in heaven above.

37　The Lord our Deliverer.

1 The Lord is our deliverer,
　Was yesterday the same.
　Through seas of Blood our Saviour
　　God [flame.
　He delivers from the fire and
　　　　CHORUS.
　My Lord delivered up Daniel
　And can't He deliver up you?

2 His windows were open toward Je-
　　rusalem, [men.
　Yet he feared not the wrath of
　For kneeling down to pray they
　　took him away,
　And put him in the lion's den.

3 David was only a Shepherd Lad,
　Yet help from Jehovah found;
　Five stones he took from a little
　　running brook
　And fell the old Giant to the
　　ground.

4 He afterward sat on a throne of
　　state,
　He was weary and often faint.
　The poor old beggar at a rich
　　man's gate,
　Was turned from a beggar to a
　　saint.

38　On the Cross.

TUNE:—"In the Cross be my Glory Ever."

1 On the Cross my Saviour died,
　Mocked, refused and hated;
　"Father, these forgive," He cried,
　"For my blood who waited."

2 On the cross He died for me,
　Me as vile as any,
　In His love, He set me free,
　Free to seek the many.

3 Like my Lord I still would bear
　All the cross He sends me;
　From the tempter's every snare,
　Still His love defends me.

4 Like my Lord, I'll live to save,
　Die to save my neighbor;
　Dying, may some wretched knave
　Bless my faithful labor.

39 My Telegram's Gone.

Wm. B. Bradbury, by per.

1. What wondrous methods God has given! Sal-va-tion wires, from earth to
2. God's tel-e-graph is strong and free, My message goes with-out a
3. I wire for God my soul to fill, I wire for power to do His
4. I wire to get the Spir-it's shower, I wire for full sal-va-tion

heaven; The Spirit's cur-rents run up there; I'll send a tel-e-
fee; God's im-age is the stamp I choose, God's promise is the
will; I wire be-fore the throne of grace, I wire to reach the
power; I wire for blood and fire to wave, I wire for God to

Chorus.

gram of prayer. My tel-e-gram's gone, . . My telegram's gone. .
form I use.
ho-ly place.
come and save.

My tel-e-gram's gone. . . My telegram's gone.

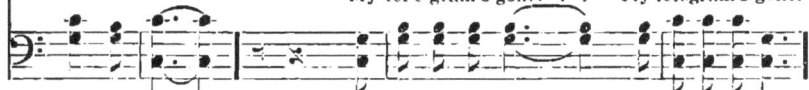

To the pal-ace of glo-ry my tel-egram's gone; My Fa-ther's

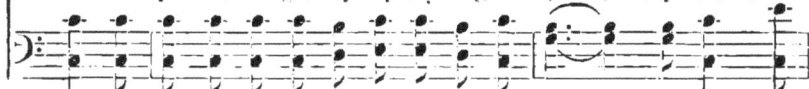

there; He'll answer prayer; My telegram's gone, my telegram's gone.

Music copyrighted, 1857, by Wm. B. Bradbury.

World of Beauty.

Mrs. ELIZABETH MILLS.

1. { I've read of a world of beauty, Where there is no gloom-y night, }
   { Where love is the mainspring of du -ty. And (*Omit*) . . . . . }
2. { I've read there is room for the weary, Who walk with the Saviour here; }
   { No mat - ter how sad or drea-ry, Is their (*Omit*) . . . . . }

CHORUS.

God is the fountain of light. I long, . . I long, . I long, yes, I
pathway with sorrow and fear.

I long, . Yes, I long,

long to be there, I long, I long, Oh yes, I long to be there.

I long, Yes, I long.

3 To rise to that world of glory,
  And breathe of its balmy air;
  To walk with the saints all holy,
  And sing with the angels there.

4 Yes, this is the hope that binds me,
  Is the path of the humble and low,
  'T is there that the Saviour doth
  find me,
  And with Him to heaven I 'll go.

41   Happy Day.
KEY OF G.

1 O happy day that fix'd my choice
  On Thee, my Saviour and my God!
  Well may this glowing heart rejoice,
  And tell its raptures all abroad.

2 O happy bond, that seals my vows,
  To Him who merits all my love;
  Let cheerful anthems fill His house
  While to that sacred shrine I
  move

3 'T is done, the great transaction 's
  done;
  I am my Lord's, and He is mine;
  He drew me, and I followed on,
  Charmed to confess the voice
  divine.

4 Now rest, my long-divided heart;
  Fixed on this blissful centre, rest;
  Nor ever from thy Lord depart:
  With Him of ev'ry good possess'd.

42 Hide Me in the Cleft of the Rock.

Arr. by E. L. K., and W. P.

1. Je - sus, lov-er of my soul, Let me to Thy bos - om fly,
2. Hide me, O my Saviour, hide, While temptations round me sweep,
3. Let no stream, however bright, Tempt my spirit from a - bove,
4. Oth-er refuge have I none, And my soul to Thee still clings;

While the sun-lit ripples roll, Not a cloud in all the sky.
Safe in - to the haven guide, And my feet from falling keep.
Or one moment to lose sight Of the o - cean of Thy love.
Cleanse and keep me as Thy own, 'Neath the shadow of Thy wings.

Chorus.

Hide, oh hide me in the cleft of the rock, Oh, hide, oh,

hide me in the cleft of the rock, Oh, hide me! Yes,

hide me Lord,

hide me, In the cleft of the rock, hide me, Lord.

hide me, Lord,

37

43   Open Wide.

Arr. by E. L. K. and W. P.

1.   I am go -ing to a home bright and fair, And by faith its pearly gates I see,
2. There's a mansion built for me over there, Soon in heav'n my dwelling place shall be,
3.   Let me hasten to my home over there, With my Saviour ev-er-more to be,
4.   Yes, I'll enter thro' the gates by the blood, Which my blessed Saviour shed for me,

Soon I'll be among the bless'd over there, For the gates are open wide for   me.
Which my Saviour now has gone to prepare, And the gates are open wide for   me.
On the wings of holy Angels a-rise, Thro' the gates that are open wide for   me.
Passing underneath the cleansing flood, Heaven's gates are open wide for   me.

CHORUS.

O -pen wide,   o-pen wide,   Yes, the gates are open wide for me.

o-pen wide,   o-pen wide,

O-pen wide,   o-pen wide,   Yes, the gates are open wide for me.

open wide,   open wide,

44   Jesus is Strong to Deliver.

J. P. W.

1. When in the tempest He'll hide us, When in the storm He'll be near;
2. When in my sor-row He found me, Found me, and bade me be whole,
3. Why are you doubting and fearing, Why are you still under sin?
4. You say, "I am weak, I am helpless, I've tried a-gain and a - gain;"

All the way 'long He will carry us on, Now we have nothing to fear.
Turn'd all my night in-to heavenly light, And from me my burden did roll.
Have you not found that His grace doth abound, He's mighty to save, let Him in!
Well, this may be true, But it's not what *you* do, "'Tis *He* who's th'···mighty to save."

CHORUS.

Je - sus is strong to de - liv - er, Might-y to save, Might-y to save!

Je -sus is strong to de - liv - er, Je -sus is might-y to save!

45   We are Coming.

1 Wanderer from Jesus, weary, sad
    and lone,   [thee,
   Hear Him gently calling now for
   Hear His precious promise to the
    erring one:
   I will love freely; come to me.

CHORUS.
We are coming, loving Saviour,
   We are coming in our wretched-
    ness and woe,
Oh receive us, Oh relieve us, [bestow.
   Do the fulness of Thy grace on us

2 He will love you freely, your back-
    slidings heal,   [day.
   He will turn your darkness into
   Pleasant paths of peace the Spirit
    will reveal,   [highway.
   He will lead you in the King's

3 Wanderer from Jesus, why not now
    return,   [stay?
   Why in sin and darkness longer
   Hasten to the feet of Jesus, there
    to learn   [Way.
   All about the Life, the Truth, the

Won't You Come Back?

C. P. B.

Changed by E. L. K.

1. O won't you come back to the fold? The Shepherd is call-ing for
2. O won't you come back to the fold? You are miss'd from the circle
3. O won't you come back to the fold? The world is cru-el and

you, And griev'd cause your heart is so cold; He knows of the good you could
of pray'r, Where with joy and peace you have told How sweet it was to be
bad, And Sa-tan has been very bold, And robbed you the grace you once

do; It was not so al-ways, you know, You
there. So don't be dis-couraged to-night; Try
had. Re-turn un-to me, saith the Lord, And

once was so ten-der and kind; The heart now has lost all its
a-gain the beau-ti-ful way, And dare to stand up for the
I will re-turn un-to you: Be do-ers just now of His

CHORUS.

glow, And eyes that did see are now blind. Wont you come back,
right, Lean all on the Sav-iour and pray.
word, Come feast as you once used to do.

Won't You Come Back? Concluded.

wont you come back, Wont you come back to the fold? The
Shepherd is call-ing for you, Oh, wont you come back to the fold?

47 Satisfied with Jesus.

Arr. by E. L. K. and W. P.

1. Am I a sol-dier of the Cross, A fol-l'wer of the Lamb, And
2. Must I be car-ried to the skies On flow-'ry beds of ease, While
3. Are there no foes for me to face? Must I not stem the flood? Is
4. Since I must fight if I would reign, Increase my courage, Lord; I'll

Cho. I'm sat - is -fied with Je-sus here, He's ev - 'ry-thing to me, His

shall I fear to own His cause, Or blush to speak His name?
oth - ers fought to win the prize, And sailed thro' bloody seas?
this vile world a friend to grace, To help me on to God?
bear the toil, endure the pain, Sup-port - ed by Thy Word.

dy - ing love has won my heart, And now He sets me free.

48 When the Roll is Called.

1. When the roll is call'd in heaven, And the host shall mus-ter there,
2. When the roll is call'd in heaven, I will an - swer to my name,
3. When the roll is call'd in heaven, To the front I'll make my way,

I will take my place among them, And their joys and triumphs share.
And come for-ward at the sum-mons My in - her - itance to claim.
And be welcomed by the Mas-ter To the realms of endless day!

CHORUS.

An-gels, call the roll up yonder, Muster day in heav'n proclaim,

Call the roll, and at the summons I will an - swer to my name.

49 Free from the Bondage.

1 I'm a happy soldier on my way to heaven, [forgiven;
Though in sin I've wandered I'm
When the Saviour saw me on the mountain cold,
He brought the wand'rer to His fold.
CHORUS.
Free from the bondage, free from the fear, [even here,
Crowned with salvation, Heaven
Shouting Hallelujah, as we march along,
Oh come and join our happy throng.

2 Since I've joined the Crusaders, bat-tles I have seen, [in;
Conflicts and temptations I've been
But the strength of Jesus, daily to me given,
Has kept me on the way to heaven.

3 Oh what peace and comfort does the hope afford, [Lord;
Soon to be in heaven with the
Then we'll shout forever, all our trials o'er,
42 And sing upon a happier shore.

50 It is Good to be Here.

C. WESLEY.

Adapted by H. T. C.

1. { O how hap - py are they, Who the Sav-iour o - bey, And have
Tongue can nev - er ex - press The sweet comfort and peace Of a

D. C. And the light streaming down makes the pathway all clear, It is

1. laid up their treasures a-bove. . (Omit). . . . . }
(Omit.) . . . . .soul in its ear - li - est love. }
(Omit.) . . . . good for us, Lord, to be here.

FINE.

CHORUS.

D. C.

It is good to be here, It is good to be here, Thy perfect love drives away fear.

2 This sweet comfort was mine,
When the favor Divine [Lamb;
I received through the blood of the
When my heart first believed,
What a joy I received —
What a heaven in Jesus' name!

3 Jesus, all the day long,
Was my joy and my song:
O that all His salvation might see;

" He hath loved me," I cried,
" He hath suffered and died,
To redeem even rebels like me."

4 O the rapturous height
Of that holy delight [blood;
Which I felt in the life-giving
Of my Saviour possessed,
I was perfectly blest,
As if filled with the fulness of God.

51 Almost Persuaded.

TUNE:—G. H. 75. Key of G.

1 " Almost persuaded " now to be-
lieve; [ceive;
" Almost persuaded " Christ to re-
Seems now some soul to say,
" Go, Spirit, go Thy way,
Some more convenient day
On Thee I'll call."

2 " Almost persuaded, " come, come
to-day; [way,
" Almost persuaded, " turn not a-
Jesus invites you here,

Angels are lingering near,
Prayers rise from hearts so dear:
" O wanderer, come. "

3 " Almost persuaded, " harvest is
past ! [at last!
" Almost persuaded, " doom comes
" Almost " cannot avail :
" Almost " is but to fail !
Sad, sad, that bitter wail —
" Almost — but lost ! "

P. P. Bliss.

43

52 Gathering Home.

I. B.   Rev. 20: 12.   Rev. I. Baltzell.

1. We'll all gather home in the morning, On the banks of the bright jasper
2. We'll all gather home in the morning, At the sound of the great ju-bi-
3. We'll all gather home in the morning, Our bless-ed Re-deem-er to

sea; We'll meet all the good and the faithful, What a gath'ring that will be!
lee; We'll all gather home in the morning; What a gath'ring that will be!
see; We'll meet with the friends gone before us; What a gath'ring that will be!

Chorus.

What a gath - 'ring, gath - 'ring,
What a gath-'ring that will be, that will be, What a

gath-'ring that will be! What a gath - 'ring,
that will be! While the an - gels sing we'll

gath - - 'ring, What a gath-'ring that will be!
all gath - er home;

53 The New Song.

H. POLLARD.
CHORUS.   Southern Melody.

1. Wait a lit-tle while, Then we'll sing the New Song,

Wait a lit-tle while, Then we'll sing the New Song.

1. When the great Ju - bi -lee shall come, Then we'll sing the New Song,

End with Chorus.

And Christ shall take His ransom'd home, Then we'll sing the New Song.

2 When the long night of sin shall
close,
Then we'll sing the New Song;
And life's fair day shall end our woes,
Then we'll sing the New Song.

3 When the glad shout shall rend the
sky,
Then we'll sing the New Song;
"O grave, where is thy victory?"
Then we'll sing the New Song.

4 When sorrow, pain, and death are
o'er,
Then we'll sing the New Song;
And sighs and tears shall be no more
Then we'll sing the New Song.

5 When to the pearly gates we come,
Then we'll sing the New Song,
When we have reached our blissful
home,
Then we'll sing the New Song.

6 When we shall tread Life's river
brink,
Then we'll sing the New Song;
And of those crystal waters drink,
Then we'll sing the New Song,

7 Where all will be immortal, fair,
There we'll sing the New Song;
When blood-washed robes are ours
to wear,
Then we'll sing the New Song.

45

The Battle of Faith.

1. The Bat - tle of faith is now be-gun, Christ is my staff and
2. The war may rage with-in my soul, And Sa - tan try his

rod, Sal - va - tion free was giv - en me, When I was born of
best, To lure me back to his old ways, But still I'll stand the

God, And tho' the tempter may suggest, Yet I can say with-in, Thy
test, For Je - sus is my guide and friend, He's promised me to keep, So

Grace is all - suf - fi - cient now, To con-quer ev - 'ry sin.
now with sim - ple faith I'll bow, Sub-mis-sive at His feet.

Chorus.

We will joy. . . . . in God a - bove, We will
And we will joy in God a - bove,

The Battle of Faith. Concluded.

joy. . . . . in God a-bove. . . . . We will

and we will joy, In God a-bove,

joy. . . . . . in God a-bove, For His

In God a-bove, In God a-bove,

gift, His won-drous gift of love, His gift of love.

55 The Crusaders with Jesus.

1 My Jesus, I love Thee, I know Thou art mine,
For Thee all the pleasures of sin I resign,
My gracious Redeemer, my Saviour art Thou,
Hallelujah, my Jesus, I love Thee just now.

CHORUS.

The Crusaders with Jesus will march hand in hand,
And the saved ones down here will be saved in that land;
We'll meet ne'er to part on that hallelujah strand.
Say, will you go; say, will you go.

2 I love Thee because Thou hast first loved me,
And purchased my pardon when nailed to the tree,
I love Thee for wearing the thorns in Thy brow,
Hallelujah, my Jesus, I love Thee just now.

3 I will love Thee in life, I will love Thee in death,
And praise Thee as long as Thou lendest me breath;
And say when the death-dew lies cold on my brow,
Hallelujah, my Jesus, I love Thee just now.

4 In mansions of glory and endless delight,
I'll ever adore Thee, and dwell in Thy sight;
I'll sing with a glittering crown on my brow,
Hallelujah, my Jesus, I love Thee just now.

56 Welcome Home.

1. With quick'ning pace the sol - diers march Towards the bliss-ful
2. Our pas - sage thro' a des - ert lies, Where fu-rious li - ons
3. When tempt-ed to for - sake his God, And give the con - test
4. When stern af - flic - tion pales our face, And death stands at the

shore, And sing, with burning, joyous hearts, "'T is better on be - fore."
roar; We fol - low Christ, and smiling say, "'T is better on be - fore."
o'er; He hears a voice which says, "Look up! 'T is better on be - fore."
door; We glad - ly say by Je - sus' grace, "'T is better on be - fore."

CHORUS.

There's a wel - come home, a wel - come home, The soldiers' welcome

home; There's a welcome home, a welcome home, The soldiers' welcome home.

5 And when in front of death we
  stand,
  We view the radiant shore,
  We'll cross the river at command;
  "'T is better on before."

6 Nor night, nor death, nor parting
  sounds,
  Can reach that healthful shore,
  But peace, and joy, and endless life;
  "'Tis better on before."

48

Fading Away.

Arr. by W. C. and W. P.

1. Lips I have kissed, they are fad-ed and cold, Hands I have clasped, they are
2. Fair were the flow'rs that bloomed in our home, Bright was their presence, sweet
3. Down where the waves of the riv - er rolled high, Sad - ly and soft - ly we
4. O - ver the stream came the boatman so pale, Came in a boat with a

covered with mould; Forms I have pressed, they have withered a - way,
their per - fume; Up to the gar - dens of beau-ti-ful day,
whispered good - by; O - ver the stream that was darker than night,
snow-y white sail; Quick-ly he bore them o-ver the foam,

CHORUS.

Gone are the dear ones, fad - ed a-way. Fad - ing a-way, to the
Softly, the Death Angel bore them a-way.
Sad - ly we saw them go out of sight.
Gone are the dear ones, gone from our home.

un - seen shore, Fad - ing a-way, they are gone be - fore;

Fad-ing a-way to the si-lent land, Fading, fad-ing a-way.

5 Soon will the shadows of earth-life be past
Sorrows and partings be over at last;
Soon we shall meet in the mansions of day,
Meet where our dear ones will ne'er fade away.

Farther On.

Arr. by E. L. K., and W. P.

1. I'm a sol-dier bound for glo-ry, I'm a sol-dier marching on;
2. I will tell you what in-duced me For the bet-ter land to start;
3. When I first with Christ en-list-ed, Ma-ny said "He'll turn a-gain;"

Come and hear me tell my sto-ry, All who long in sin have gone.
'Twas the Sav-iour's lov-ing kindness O-ver-came and won my heart.
But tho' ev-'ry day re-sist-ed, In the ranks I still re-main.

CHORUS.

Far-ther on, yes still far-ther, Count the mile-stones one by one;

Je-sus will for-sake you nev-er, It is bet-ter far-ther on.

4 I'm a wonder unto many,
   God alone the change hath wrought;
   Here I raise my " Ebenezer,"
   Hither by His help I'm brought.

5 Soon to Jordan's swelling river,
   Like a soldier I shall come;
   Then I mean to shout Salvation
   And go singing glory home.

59 Seek the Joys of Heaven's Home.

Arr. by E. L. K. and W. P.

1. There is none but Je-sus, sin-ner, None to help you, none to save.
2. You have struggled long to find it, And at times you pleasure had,
3. You have prov'd that worldly pleasure Ends in sorrow, pain, re-morse,
4. For the soldier of King Je-sus, There is perfect peace and love,
5. Now, dear sinner, ask the Saviour To forgive and pardon you.

Do not trust this world for pleasure; Seek the joys of heaven's home.
But you ne'er found satisfaction; Seek the joys of heaven's home.
Seek no more such costly gladness, Seek the joys of heaven's home.
There is all that he can wish for And the joy of go-ing home.
He will gladly cleanse and fit you, For that bright and heav'nly home.

Chorus.

Seek the joys of heaven's home. Seek the joys of heaven's home,

Do not trust this world for pleasure, Seek the joys of heaven's home.

60 Jesus is Mine.

1 Fade, fade each earthly joy;
   Jesus is mine.
Break every tender tie;
   Jesus is mine.
Dark is the wilderness,
Earth has no resting-place;
Jesus alone can bless;
   Jesus is mine.

2 Tempt not my soul away;
   Jesus is mine.
Here would I ever stay;
   Jesus is mine.

Perishing things of clay,
Born but for one brief day,
Pass from my heart away;
   Jesus is mine.

3 Farewell, ye dreams of night;
   Jesus is mine.
Lost in this dawning light;
   Jesus is mine.
All that my soul hath tried
Left but a dismal void —
Jesus has satisfied;
   Jesus is mine.

61 The Half has Never been Told.

FRANCES RIDLEY HAVERGAL. 1 Cor. 2: 9. R. E. HUDSON.

1. I know I love Thee better, Lord, Than a-ny earth-ly joy, For
2. I know that Thou art nearer still Than a-ny earth-ly throng, And
3. Thou hast put gladness in my heart; Then well may I be glad! With-
4. O Saviour, precious Saviour mine! What will Thy presence be If

Thou hast giv-en me the peace Which noth-ing can de-stroy.
sweet-er is the tho't of Thee Than a-ny love-ly song.
out the se-cret of Thy love I could not but be sad.
such a life of joy can crown Our walk on earth with Thee?

CHORUS.

The half has nev-er yet been told, (yet been told,) Of love so full and free;

The half has never yet been told, (yet been told,) The blood it cleanseth me. (cleanseth me.)

rit.

62 I Believe We shall Win.

1 We've a band that shall conquer the foe, [King,
If we fight in the strength of the
With the Sword of the Spirit we know
We shall sinners to Calvary bring.

CHORUS.

I believe we shall win, we shall win,
If we fight in the strength of the King.

2 We have conquered in times that are past, [the field,
And we've scattered the foe from
Then we'll fight for the King till the last, [wield.
And the Sword of the Spirit we'll

3 Our foe may be mighty and brave,
And the fighting be hard and se-vere,
But the King is the mighty to save,
And in conflict He always is near.

63 Sunlight for the Soul.

Arr. by E. L. K. and W. P.

1. When Je-sus died on Cal-va-ry, To bring sunlight to our souls, He
2. I hear the voice of Je-sus say, Here is sun-light for thy soul, Cast
3. He bore my sin, and curse and shame, Bringing sunlight to my soul; You
4. And when the fighting all is o'er, With the sunlight in my soul, I'll

suf-fered there for you and me, There is sun-light for your soul.
ev-'ry sin and fear a-way, Here is sun-light for thy soul.
may be sav'd thro' Je-sus' name, With the sun-light in your soul.
sing up-on the gold-en shore, Of the sun-light in my soul.

Chorus.

There is sun - - - light, bless-ed sun - - - light, While the

There is sun-light in my soul, bless - ed sunlight in my soul,

peace-ful happy moments roll, When Je-sus shows His

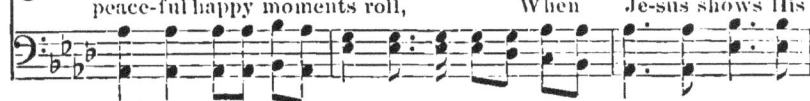

mo-ments roll,

smil - ing face, There is sun - light in my soul.

No Redemption.

Arr. by W. P. and E. L. K.

1. Come, sin-ner, I've something to tell you; Come near while I whisper it
2. The joys of this world have inducements To trap both the young and the
3. The Bankers and Brokers are wealthy, They are making their millions

low, I've started to meet my dear Saviour, Up there where I'm longing to go.
old. But heav'n by faith is a city, Whose portals are gleam-ing with gold.
or more, But riches can never be carried Beyond death's cold, wide open door.

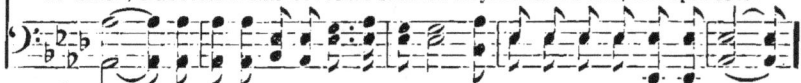

CHORUS.

Come un - to the Saviour, He's waiting, Come seek Him, He's mighty to

save; Remem-ber there is no re-demp-tion Beyond the cold walls of the grave.

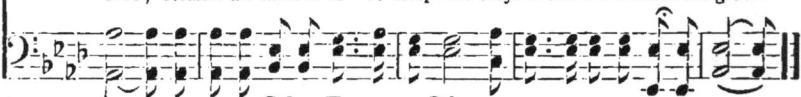

65   Oh Poor Sinner.

1 The twilight shades of evening gather,
And the light of life grows dim,
There's thousands dying now in sor-row,
And millions steeped in sin.
No chiming bells, no joyous sound
To break that hellish spell,
Who'll do or dare, who'll volunteer,
To save these souls from hell?
Chorus.
Oh poor sinner, oh poor sinner,
What will you do on that day,
When the stars shall fall and the heavens part,
And the earth shall pass away?

2 Art thou among the godless num-ber
Who are drifting to their doom,
Whose souls are dashed on sin's rough mountain,
Who are living in a dream;
No cheering hope to help them on-ward
Along life's weary path,
Thou art living, eating, sleeping, drinking,
Enwrapt in the arms of death.

3 There's hope for thee, my wayward brother
And sister too, for thee;
I hear a voice which speaks from heav'n
And says thy soul I'll free.
'Tis the voice of Christ, the world's redeemer,
Who comes from heaven down,
Take courage now and claim the promise,
And thou shalt wear a crown.

Home Once More.

1. I'm a prod - i - gal come home, Nev-er more to stray or roam,
2. My Saviour's voice I hear, With His accents soft and clear,
3. Though storms may beat a-round, I have full Sal - va-tion found;
4. When my journ-ey here is o'er, And I reach the gold-en shore,

Midst the surges and the breakers of this world, And my heart with
Gent - ly whispering peace and comfort to my soul; Saying, child be
On the Rock of A-ges now I take my stand, And one day I
Where the ransomed of the Lord in glo - ry dwell. There where friends have

joy doth bound, For I know the lost is found; I'm a prod - i -
of good cheer, I am with you, do not fear; And the an - gels
shall be crowned In the City to which I'm bound; I'm a prod - i -
gone be - fore I will sing for - ev - er - more; I'm a prod - i -

CHORUS.

gal come to his home once more. . . Home once more, home once
sing a welcome home once more. . .
gal come to his home once more. . .
gal come to his home once more. . .

more, A prodigal returned to his home once more, I've left the way of

sin the Devil held me in, And glo-ry be to God, I'm home once more.

Sing it o 'er Again.

1 Christ accepts me, now I'm free,
Now I've peace and liberty;
Grace abounds on every land,
Till I reach the better land.

CHORUS.
Sing it o'er and o'er again.

2 Vile with sin and full of doubt,
Jesus did not cast me out;

In my grief and misery,
He just said, "Come unto Me."

3 For Him ever I will live,
Time and talents to Him give;
He's my strength from day to day,
While I march my heavenward
way.

4 Grace proportioned to my day,
And His eyes to guide my way;
May I ever faithful be,
To the Lord, who died for me.

1. Come shout and sing, make heaven ring, With praise to our King, Who bled and died, was
2. Come join our band and make a stand, To drive sin from our land; To do or die is our
3. At trumpet's sound, we stand our ground, And tell to those around, Who have been long with

crucified, That He might pardon bring, His blood doth save the soul, cleanse
battle cry, We fight at God's command, With ban-ner wide unfurled, we tell
shackles strong, By sin and Satan bound. Sal-va - tion God has sent, for all

and make it whole, The blood of Jesus cleanses white as snow. .
to all the world, The blood of Jesus cleanses white as snow. .
who will re - pent, The blood of Jesus cleanses white as snow. .

CHORUS.

The blood of Jesus cleanses white as snow; don't you know? The blood of Jesus

cleanses white as snow; I've proved it so, Oh, bless the hap-py day, He

The Blood of Jesus. Concluded.

washed my sins a-way, The blood of Jesus cleanses white as snow.

69   Swing those Gates Ajar!

1. { Oh, good old way, how sweet thou art, Swing those gates a - jar!
{ But may our ac-tions al-ways say, Swing those gates a - jar!

May none of us from Thee de-part, Swing those gates a - jar! }
We're marching in the good old way, Swing those gates a - jar! }

Chorus

Swing them o - pen, An-gels, Swing them wide and far; The bells do ring, the

An-gels sing, Swing those gates a - jar, Swing them o - pen, An - gels,

Swing them wide and far; The bells do ring, the angels sing Swing those gates ajar.

2 Above the rest this note shall swell,
That Jesus doeth all things well.
I mean to hear Him say "well done,"
And then go singing "glory home."

3 I don't care where they bury me,
If on the land or in the sea;
For when the fighting all is o'er;
I'll rest upon the golden shore.

57

Calvary's Stream is Flowing.

Arr. by W. P. and E. L. K.

1. In e - vil long I took de - light, Unawed by shame or fear,
2. I saw one hanging on a tree, In ag - o - nies and blood.
3. Sure nev-er till my lat-est breath, Can I forget that look;
4. My conscience felt and owned my guilt, And plunged me in de - spair,
5. A sec-ond look he gave, which said, "I free - ly all for - give;

Till a new ob-ject met my sight, And stopped my wild ca- reer.
Who fixed His lan-guid eyes on me, As near the cross I stood.
It seemed to charge me with His death, Tho' not a word He spoke.
I saw my sins His blood had spilt, And helped to nail Him there.
This blood is for thy ransom paid, I die that thou may'st live."

CHORUS.

Calvary's stream is flow - ing, Calvary's stream is flow - ing.

Flow-ing so free for you and me; Calvary's stream is flow-ing.

71 Sinking out of Self.

1 Now crucified with Christ I am
The self within is slain,
But still I live and yet not I,
Christ lives in me again.

CHORUS.

I am sinking out of self, out of self
into Christ,
Sinking out of self into Christ,
I am sinking, sinking, sinking out
of self,
Sinking out of self into Christ.

2 Dead to the world and sin I am,
Alive to God alone,
The life I have I live by faith,
In God's beloved Son,

3 The throne of self within my heart,
The king of saints doth fill
My spirit crowns Lord of all,
And waits to do his will.

4 Hereafter it is no more I,
Nor sin that ruleth me,
Reign, reign forever blessed Lord,
My all I give to Thee.

Blessed Jesus.

Air: — ' RAISE ME, JESUS."

1. When the sol - emn shad - ows dark - en, And my
2. By Thy pas - sion in the gar - den, By Thine
CHO. *Bless - ed Je - sus, Gra - cious Sav - iour, When the*

wea - ry spir - it sighs, Ho - ly Sav-iour, wilt Thou
an - guish on the tree, By that pre-cious gift of
night grows still and deep, Let us in Thine arms re -

heark - en, As Thy children's pray'rs a-rise? Some are tried with
par - don, Set the sin-bound captive free. Some in con - flict
pos - ing, Feel Thy pow'r to save and keep.

doubts and fearing, Some have found their hearts grow cold; Some are
sore have striv-en, With temp-ta-tion fierce and strong; So to

a - liens now and strangers To the faith they lov'd of old.
them let strength be giv - en, Change their mourning in -to song.

73 Welcome to Glory.

Mrs. P. Palmer.   Mrs. J. F. Knapp.

1. O, when shall I sweep thro' the gate, The scenes of mortal-i-ty o'er,
2. When from Calvary's mount I arise, And pass thro' the portals a-bove,
3. Yes! loved ones who knew me below, Who learned the new song with me here,
4. The beau-ti-ful gates will un-fold, The home of the blood-washed I'll see;
5. A sin-ner made whiter than snow, I'll join in the might-y ac-claim,

What then for my spir-it awaits? Will they sing on the glo-ri-fied shore?
Will shouts, Welcome home to the skies! Re-sound thro' the regions of love?
In cho-rus will hail me, I know, And welcome me home, with good cheer
The cit-y of saints I'll be-hold! For, O, there's a welcome for me!
And shout thro' the gates as I go, Sal-va-tion to God and the Lamb!

Chorus.

Welcome home! welcome home! A wel-come in glo-ry for
Welcome home! Welcome home!

me; Welcome home! welcome home! A welcome for me.
Welcome home! Welcome home! Welcome home!

74 Where is My Boy To-Night?

1 Where is my wand'ring boy to-night?
The boy of my tenderest care,
The boy that was once my joy and light,
The child of my love and pray'r?

Chorus.

O where is my boy to-night?
O where is my boy to-night?
My heart o'erflows, for I love him, he knows,
O where is my boy to-night?

3 Once he was pure as morning dew,
As he knelt at his mother's knee;
No face was so bright, no heart more true
And none was so sweet as he.

3 O could I see you now, my boy,
As fair as in olden time, [a joy,
When prattle and smile made home
And life was a merry chime!

4 Go for my wand'ring boy to-night;
Go search for him where you will;
But bring him to me with all his blight,
And tell him I love him still.

60

75 Redeemed by His Blood.

J. M. SAWERS.   I. John 1: 17.   J. M. SAWERS.

1. Oh, the blood, the precious blood, Glory to Je-sus, I
2. I'm glad the blood has reach'd my soul, Happy in Je-sus, and
3. Hal-le-lu-jah to Jesus, His praise I'll sing, Hark! how the heaven-ly

plunged in the flood; Now I'm rest-ing on His word, En-
ev-'ry whit whole; Now the "old chariot" I'll help to roll, En-
joy - bells ring: Glo - ry, hon - or, praise and pow'r To

joy - ing a full sal - va - tion.   Re - deemed, . . re-
joy - ing a full sal - va - tion.
Him . . who bro't sal - va - tion.

CHORUS.

deemed, Re-deemed by His pre - cious, cleans-ing blood; Re -

deemed, re - deemed, Re -deemed by His pre -cious blood.

Never Alone!

Words and adaption by WILLIAM PROCTER.

1. I've seen the light-'nings flashing, And heard the thun-ders roll;
2. The world's fierce winds are blowing Tempta - tions sharp and keen—
3. When in af - flic - tion's val - ley I'm treading the road of care,
4. He died for me on the mountain; For me they pierc'd His side;

I've felt sin's breakers dash-ing,   Trying to conquer my soul:
I feel a peace in know-ing   My Sa-viour stands be-tween:
The Sav-iour helps me to car-ry   My cross when heavy to bear;
For me He open'd that fountain,   The crim - son, cleansing tide:

I heard the voice of my Sav - iour, Tell-ing me still to fight on:
He stands to shield me from dan-ger, When earthly friends are gone:
My feet, en-tangled with bri - ars, Read-y to cast me down:
For me He's waiting in glo - ry, Seat-ed up - on His throne:

He promised never to leave me—Nev-er to leave me a - lone!
He promised never to leave me—Nev-er to leave me a - lone!
My Sav-iour whispers His prom-ise—Nev-er to leave me a - lone!
He promised never to leave me—Nev-er to leave me a - lone!

CHORUS.

No, nev-er a - lone! .. No, nev-er a - lone! .. He

Nev-er a-lone!   Nev-er a-lone!

Never Alone! Concluded.

prom-ised nev-er to leave me— No, nev-er a-lone!

77 I'm Going Home.

E. L. KNOWLTON.

1 Now I can read my ti-tle clear to a mansion in the sky; I've
2 Should earth against my soul engage, And fier-y darts be hurl'd; Bold
3 In heav'n I'll bathe my happy soul In seas of heav'n-ly rest, And

said good-by to ev-'ry fear, And wip'd my weep-ing eyes.
I can smile at sa-tan's rage, And face a frowning world.
hear the songs of vic-t'ry roll From ev-'ry com-rade's breast.

CHORUS.   rit.

I'm go-ing home, I'm going home, To Heaven when I die; I'll

a tempo.

walk around those "Golden streets" In that land beyond the sky.

78 — Jesus is Coming.

Arr. by E. L. K.

1. Sin - ners, whith-er will you wan-der, whith - er will you stray?
2. Sa - tan has resolved to have you for his law-ful prey;
3. List - en to the in - vi - ta-tion, while He's crying, "come,"

O re-mem - ber life is slen-der, 't is but a short day.
Je - sus Christ has died to save you: haste, O haste a - way.
If you miss the great sal-va - tion, hell will be your doom.

CHORUS.

Christ is com - ing, sure - ly com - ing, and the judg-ment day,

Hast - en, sin - ner, to re-pentance; seek the nar-row way.

4 Soon you'll see the Lord descending on His great white throne,
Saints and sinners all attending to receive their doom.

5 Would you 'scape the awful sentence? from destruction flee;
Seek the Lord by true repentance, haste to Calvary.

79 — Come, Jesus.

1 Come, Jesus, Lord, with holy fire,
Come, and my quickened heart
inspire,
Cleansed in Thy precious blood.
Now to my soul Thyself reveal,
Thy mighty working let me feel,
Since I am born of God.

2 Let nothing now my heart divide,
Since with Thee I am crucified,
And live to God in Thee.
Dead to the world and all its toys
Its idle pomp and fading joys,
Jesus, my glory be.

3 Me with a quenchless thirst inspire,
A longing, infinite desire,
And fill my craving heart.
Less than Thyself, oh, do not give;
In might Thyself within me live:
Come, all Thou hast and art.

4 My will be swollowed up in Thee,
Light in Thy light still may I see,
In Thine unclouded face:
Called the full strength of trust to
prove,
Let all my quickened heart be love,
My spotless life be praise,

64

Why I love My Jesus.

E. A. HOFFMAN.

1. Would you know why I love Je - sus? Why he is so dear to me?
2. Would you know why I love Je - sus? Why he is so dear to me?
3. Would you know why I love Je - sus? Why he is so dear to me?

'T is be-cause my bless-ed Je - sus From my sins has ransomed me.
'T is be-cause the blood of Je - sus Ful-ly saves and cleanses me.
'T is be-cause, a - mid temp-ta-tion, He supports and strengthens me.

CHORUS.

This is why . . . . . I love my Je - - sus, This is
This is why I love my Je-sus, This is why I love him so, This is

why . . . . I love Him so; He a - toned . . .
why I love my Je-sus, This is why I love Him so; He has pardoned my trans-

. . for my transgres - sions, He has washed me white as snow.
gressions, He has pardoned my transgressions, He has washed me, He has wash'd me
white as snow.

4 Would you know why I love Jesus?
Why He is so dear to me?
'T is because in every conflict
Jesus gives me victory.

5 Would you know why I love Jesus?
Why He is so dear to me?
'T is because my friend and Saviour
He will ever, ever be.

81 I Am Free.

E. A. H.   Rev. B. C. OYLER.

1. { Now the chains of sin are brok-en, I am free, I'm free; }
   { Christ the word of pow'r has spok-en, Un-to me, to me. }
2. { Soon as I by faith received Him, Fled the night, the night; }
   { In the mo-ment I believed Him, Came the light, the light. }

CHORUS.

Hal-le-lu-jah! hal-le-lu-jah! Je-sus died for
me; Hal-le-lu-jah! hal-le-lu-jah! I am free, I'm free.

3 All the fetters that oppressed me
   Now are riven, are riven; [me,
   With His precious love He blessed
   This to me is heaven.

4 I will tell the wondrous story
   Of His grace and love;
   He has filled my soul with glory,
   Praise the Lord above!

82 Let Him In.

1 Love of Love is wondrous,
   Rich and free;
   Now the King of glory
   A pardon offers thee.

   CHORUS.
   Now He is waiting, pleading, knock-
   Let Him in, [ing,
   He is waiting, pleading, knocking,
   Let Him in.

2 For thy heart He's waited
   Days and years,

And thy sins long hated
   Have caused Him bitter tears.

3 Can'st thou leave His pardon
   Still unknown.
   And forget the mercy
   That towards thee He has shown.

4 Soon the day is coming,
   When alone,
   Trembling or rejoicing
   You must His kingship own.

83 Boundless Love.

1 Jesus stands and knocks and pleads,
   Calling for the wanderer home,
   And for sinners He intercedes,
   Calling for the wanderer home.

   CHORUS.
   Boundless love beyond degree,
   Calling for the wanderer home,
   Jesus longs to set you free,
   Calling for the wanderer home,

2 As a lamb to slaughter led,
   On the cross His blood was shed,
   He has often called before,
   Now He's waiting at the door.

3 Come, oh come, while yet He
   stands, [hands,
   While in love He spreads His
   Soon His mercy will be o'er
   66   Thou shalt hear His voice no more.

84 The Pearly Gate.

"Strive to enter in at the strait gate."

Ellen Oliver.

E. B. Smith.

DUET.

1. The door of God's mercy is o-pen   To all who are weary of sin,
2. The world is e'er wantonly wooing Your soul from the ways of the blest
3. So ma - ny who hear the glad message, Will nev-er its mandates o - bey,
4. Sad hearts there will surely be moaning Out-side of the gate-way of life,
5. The door of God's mercy is o-pen,   In - vit-ing-ly o - pen to all,

And   Je - sus is pa-tient-ly waiting, Still waiting, to welcome you in.
But   Je - sus is ten-der-ly bidding You turn to His heaven-ly rest.
But turn from the precious, dear pleadings, And wil-ful-ly wan-der a - way.
And pray-ing to Him they re-ject- ed When earth with gay pleasure was rife.
Who list to the voice of the Master, And hearing shall heed His sweet call.

CHORUS.

Come, says the Saviour, Come enter the gate,   I watch by the portals both

ear - ly and late, Lest some precious soul, Not far from the goal, Should

wand-er away into darkness and hate, And miss it for-ev-er, the pearly gate.

Be in Time.

Changed by E. L. K.

1. Life at best is ver-y brief, Like the fall-ing of a leaf, Like the
2. Fair-est flowers soon decay, Youth and beauty pass away, Oh, you
3. Time is glid-ing swiftly by, Death and judgment drawing nigh, To the

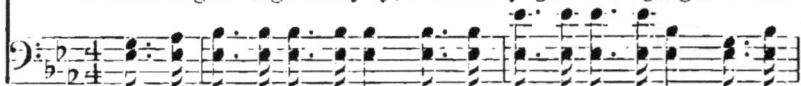

bind-ing of a sheaf; Be in time. Fleeting days are telling fast, That the
have not long to stay; Be in time. While the Spirit bids you come, Sinner,
arms of Je-sus fly; Be in time. O, I pray you, count the cost, Ere the

D. S. sin you longer wait, You may

FINE.

die will soon be cast, And the fa-tal line be past, Be in time.
do not long-er roam, Lest you seal your hopeless doom, Be in time.
fa - tal line be cross'd And your soul in hell be lost, Be in time.

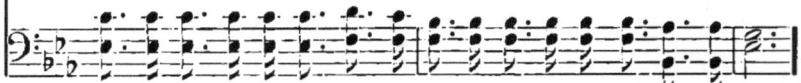

find no o-pen gate, But your sad cry be " Too late;" Be in time.

CHORUS.

Be in time, Be in time, While the voice of Jesus calls you

Be in time, be in time,

D. S.

Be in time. If in

Be in time.

4 Sinner, heed the warning voice,
  Make the Lord your final choice,
  Then all heaven will rejoice,
    Be in time.
  Come from darkness into light;
  Come, let Jesus set you right;
  Come and start for heaven to-night,
    Be in time.

86 Beautiful, Beckoning Hands.

C. C. LUTHER.　　　　　　　　　　　　　　E. L. KNOWLTON.

1. Beck - on-ing hands at the gateway to - night, Fa - ces a-shining with
2. Beck - on-ing hands of a moth-er, whose love Sac - rificed life its de-
3. Beck - on-ing hands of a lit - tle one—see, Ba - by voice calling. Oh
4. Beck - on-ing hands of a hus-band or wife, Wait-ing and watching the

ra - di - ant light; Eyes looking down from yon heav-en - ly home,
vo - tion to prove; Hands of a fa - ther, to mem-o - ry dear,
moth-er! to thee; Ro - sy-cheek'd darling, the light of our home,
lov'd ones of life; Hands of a broth - er, a sis - ter, or friend,

REFRAIN.

Beau - ti - ful hands they are beck - oning "come". Beau-ti - ful hands,
Beck'-ning up high - er the wait-ing ones here.
Tak - en so ear - ly, is beck - oning, come.
Out from the gate - way to-night they ex-tend.

Beck - on-ing hands, Call - ing the dear ones to heav-en - ly lands;

Beau - tiful hands, beckoning hands, Beautiful, beauti-ful, beckoning hands.

5 Brightest and best of that glorious throng,
Centre of all, and the theme of our song,
Jesus, our Saviour, the piercèd one stands,
Lovingly calling with beckoning hands.

69

Ye Would Not.

Luke 13: 34.

Slow.

1. I've knock'd at your heart's door often, I have pled with you o'er and o'er; And the
2. I've knock'd when you were in trouble, I have knock'd when you lay in pain, And you
3. How kind is our Saviour knocking, When we've lived so long in sin; If you'll

more I'd plead, poor lost one, The firm-er you'd fasten the door, Ah! your
promis'd sometime you'd open, But that promise was all in vain. Very
knock once more, dear Saviour, I glad-ly will let you in. Ah! you

pleasures will van-ish and with-er, Your hopes be blighted and gone; And the
soon life's breath will leave you, Your bod-y sleep 'neath the sod; As He
promis'd, lost soul, once too often, I'm gone from your door evermore! Oh,

last trump sound from heaven On the Res-ur-rection morn! And the morn!
knocks just now, do o-pen, And prepare to meet thy God, As He God.
Christ! I'm lost for-ev-er, I've to meet an an-gry God! Oh, God.

Chorus.

Ye would not, ye would not, Ye would not let me in; How

70

Ye Would Not. Concluded.

rit.

oft, I'd redeem'd you from bondage, But ye would not let me in!

88 When the Mists have Rolled Away.

ANNIE HERBERT.   E. L. KNOWLTON.

1. When the mists have rolled in splendor   From the beauty of the hills, And the
2. Oft we tread the path before us   With a wea-ry burdened heart; Oft we
3. We shall come with joy and glad-ness, We shall gather round the throne; Face to

sun light falls   in gladness   On the riv-er   and   the rills;
toil a - mid   the shad-ows,   And our fields are far   a - part;
face with those that love us,   We shall know as we   are known:

We re-call our Father's promise   In the rain-bow of   the
But the Saviour's "Come ye blessed!"   All our la - bor will   re -
And the song of our   redemption   Shall resound thro' end-less

spray. We shall know each other bet-ter   When the mists have rolled a-way.
pay When we gath -er in the morning   Where the mists have rolled a-way.
day, When the shad-ows have departed   And the mists have rolled a-way.

71

Who's that Knocking?

E. L. KNOWLTON.

1. You have oft heard the call to sur-ren - der, God's Spirit with you oft has
2. His voice you have long dis-card - ed, Un-heed-ed He's knocked at the
3. There's a time coming on when you'll want Him, To bear you safe o-ver death's
4. When He comes as a bridegroom at mid - night, No time to prepare you will

striv'n; Now, a - gain to your heart He is call - ing, And an -
door, Sin-ner, now o - pen wide to the Sav - iour, Lest He
stream; Then be wise and in time seek His fa - vor, And just
find, Then you'll knock, but in vain, for ad- mit- tance, He will

CHORUS.

oth -er blest of - fer is giv'n. Oh! who's that knocking at the
leave there to knock nev-er more.
now, while He knocks let Him in.
leave you in dark-ness be - hind.

door? Oh! who's that knocking at the door? 'T is
At the door? at the door?

rit.

Je-sus there, oh, sin-ner, hear, Let Him in while He's waiting at the door.

72

90 In the Rifted Rock.

DUET.   Arr. by E. L. K. and W. P.

1. In the Rifted Rock I'm resting, Surf is dashing at my feet;
2. Many a stormy sea I've traversed, Many a tempest shock have known,
3. Yet I now have found a haven Nev-er mov'd by tempest shock,

Storm-clouds black are o'er me hov - 'ring,   Yet my rest is all complete.
Have been driven without an -chor,   O'er the barren shores alone.
Where my soul is safe for-ev - er,   In the blessed Rifted Rock.

CHORUS.

In the Rifted Rock I'm rest-ing, Safe and sure from all a - larm,

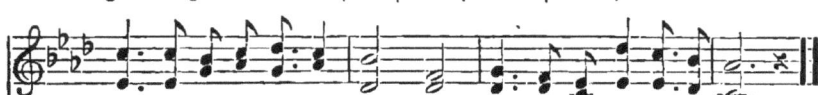

Storms and billows have u - nit - ed   All in vain to do me harm.

91 God be with You.

1 God be with you till we meet again,
By His counsels guide, uphold you,
With His sheep securely fold you,
God be with you till we meet again.

CHORUS.
Till we meet, till we meet,
Till we meet at Jesus' feet,
Till we meet, till we meet,
God be with you till we meet again.

2 God be with you till we meet again,
'Neath His wings securely fold you,
Daily manna still provide you,
God be with you till we meet again.

3 God be with you till we meet again,
When life's perils thick confound you,
Put His arms unfailing round you,
God be with you till we meet again.

4 God be with you till we meet again,
Keep His banner floating o'er you,
Smite death's treacherous wave before you,
God be with you till we meet again.

92 The Loving Shepherd.

"I am the good Shepherd; the good Shepherd giveth His life for the sheep."—*John* 10: 11.

W. A. OGDEN.   Changed by E. L. K.

1. Je - sus, the lov - ing Shep-herd, Calleth thee now to come
2. Je - sus, the lov - ing Shepherd, Gave His dear life for thee,
3. Lin-ger-ing is but fol - ly, Wolves are abroad to - day,

In - to the fold of safe - ty, Where there is rest and room.
Ten - der-ly now He's call-ing, Wan - der - er, come to Me.
Seeking the sheep who're straying, Seeking the lambs to slay.

Come in the strength of man-hood, Come in the morn of youth,
Haste, for with-out is dan - ger, Come, cries the Shepherd blest,
Je - sus, the lov - ing Shepherd, Call - eth thee now to come

En - ter the fold of safe - ty, En - ter the way of truth.
En - ter the fold of safe - ty, En - ter the place of rest.
In - to the fold of safe - ty, Where there is rest and room.

CHORUS. ARRANGED.

Lov-ing-ly, tender-ly, calling is He; Wanderer, wanderer, come un-to Me.

The Loving Shepherd. Concluded.

Patiently waiting, there standing I see, Jesus, my Shepherd di - vine.

93 Hasten to the Rescue.

Arr. by W. P.

1. In the slums of sin and mis-'ry, See the wretched drunkard reel,
2. See the drunkard's home and family, See his wretched wife in tears,
3. Go then now in - to the highways, Go and tell them God is love,

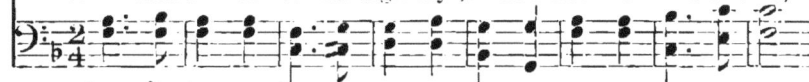

Knowing not the love of Je-sus, Oh, the anguish He must feel;
Then the cold and starv-ing children, Oh how gloom-y all ap-pears;
Talk of Him in lanes and by-ways, Bring them man-na from a-bove.

See him ly - ing in the gut - ter, Car-ing not for home or wife,
Not a ray of light is shining, Naught but sorrow, pain, and woe,
Go in-vite them to the sup-per, Call them to the mansions bright,

Cho. Hast - en, com - rades, to the res - cue, Hast - en, all ye friends of God,

Bound by rum, that hell - ish fet-ter, Curs-ing such a blight-ed life.
Comrade, can you see them dy-ing, And not to the res-cue go?
Bid them gently leave their sorrow, Turn from darkness in-to light.
To the work and He will bless you, Go and preach His lov - ing word.

75

94 So Wondrously Redeemed.

E. A. Hoffman.

E. L. Knowlton.

1. The joy I feel to - day No mor -tal could have dreamed; My
2. No more I serve the world; How sweet its pleas-ures seemed! I
3. With-in my hap -py heart The heav'n-ly light is beamed, And

heart is full of song, My heart is full of song, . . For
fol-low now my Lord, I fol-low now my Lord, . . By
I have woudrous love, And I have wondrous love, . . For

and praise,
and Christ,
and peace,

and praise,
and Christ,
and peace,

I have been re - deemed, So won-drous-ly re - deemed.
whom I am re - deemed, So won-drous-ly re - deemed.
I have been re - deemed, So won-drous-ly re - deemed.

Chorus.

Re - deemed, re -deemed, So won-drous -ly redeemed, Re-

I am redeemed, Hal -le - lu - jah.

deemed, re - deemed, So wondrously re - deemed.

I am re-deemed, Hal -le - lu - jah!

95 Home at Last.

FANNY J. CROSBY. M. LINDSAY. Arr. by W. J. K.

1. Hark the song of holy rapture, Hear it break from yonder strand,
2. Oh, the long and sweet re-union, Where the bells of time shall cease,
3. Look beyond, the skies are clearing; See, the mist dissolves away;

Where our friends for us are wait-ing, In the gold-en sum-mer land;
Oh, the greeting, endless greeting, On the ver - nal heights of peace;
Soon our eyes will catch the dawning Of a bright ce- les-tial day;

They have reached the port of glo - ry, O'er the Jordan they have passed,
Where the hop-ing and despond - ing, Of the weary heart are past,
Soon the shadows will be lift - ed That around us now are cast,

And with millions they are shouting, Home at last, home at last:
And we en - ter life e - ter-nal,—Home at last, home at last:
And re-joic - ing we shall gather Home at last, home at last:

rit.

And with mil-lions they are shouting, Home at last, home at last.
And we en - ter life e - ter-nal,— Home at last, home at last.
And re- joic - ing we shall gather Home at last, home at last.

Calvary! Dark Calvary!

Luke 23: 33.   H. R. PALMER.

1. When I sur - vey . . . the wondrous cross, . . On which the
2. On Cal-v'ry's brow . . . my Saviour died, . . 'T was there my
3. See from his head, . . . his hands, his feet, . . Sorrow and
4. 'Mid rending rocks . . . and dark'ning skies, . . My Saviour
5. O Je - sus Lord, . . . how can it be . . That Thou shouldst

Prince . . of Glory died, . . My richest gain . . I count but
Lord . . was cruci- fied, . . 'T was on the cross . . He bled for
love . . flow mingled down; . Did e'er such love, . and sorrow
bows . . His head and dies: . The op'ning veil . reveals the
give . . Thy life for me; . . To bear the cross . . and agon-

loss . . . And pour contempt . . on all my pride. . . .
me . . . And purchased there . . my pardon free. . . .
meet, . . Or thorns compose . . so rich a crown? . . .
way . . . To heaven's joys . . and endless day. . . .
y, . . . In that dread hour . . on Calva - ry! . . .

Chorus.

O Cal-va-ry! dark Calvary! My longing heart is turned to thee; O

Cal - va-ry! dark Cal - va-ry! Speak to my heart from Calva-ry.

We 'll Fight.

Arr. by W. P.

1. O Lord, on Thee our care we cast, Our labors Thou hast blest ; Sal-
2. The best for light, for ho - ly might, For skill to guide the war ; For
3. The best for wisdom, pow'r, and grace, For feeling Heaven near, For

va-tion years have brightly passed, Lord let this be the best, Lord let this be the best.
war-riors such as in the fight, Thy Soldiers never saw, Thy soldiers nev-er saw.
room and place the foe to chase, For victory ev-ery-where, For vic-tory ev-ery-where.

CHORUS.

We'll fight, we'll fight, we'll fight, we'll fight, we'll fight, the bat-tle through ; Our

path-way clear, and let this year Be the best we ev - er knew, Be the

best we ev - er knew.

4 The best to work, the best to live,
   The best to speak and sing :
The best to pray, to get, to give,
   More cheerful gifts to bring.

5 The best for Soldiers saved from
     fear,
   For servants who'll obey ;
Who'll help the crusade every year,
   Who'll help it night and day.

98 Lead Me Gently Home, Father.

Words and Music by WILL L. THOMPSON.

1. Lead me gently home, Father, Lead me gently home, When life's toils are ended, and
2. Lead me gently home, Father, Lead me gently home; In life's darkest hours, Father,

parting days have come; Sin no more shall tempt me, Ne'er from Thee I'll
When life's troubles come, Keep my feet from wand'ring, Lest from Thee I

rit. p

roam,   If Thou'lt on-ly lead me, Fa-ther, Lead me gently home.
roam,   Lest I fall up-on the way side, Lead me gently home.

CHORUS.

Lead   me gen-tly   home,   Fa-ther, Lead me gen-tly
Lead me gently home,   Fa-ther, Lead me gently   home, Fa-ther,

Lead Me Gently Home, Father. Concluded.

Lest I fall up-on the way-side, Lead me gen-tly home.
Lead me gen-tly, gen - tly home.

99 Prepare Me.

CHORUS.

rall. FINE.

Pre-pare me! pre-pare me, Lord! Prepare me to stand before Thy throne.

rall. D.S.

1. { Your garments must be white as snow, Prepare to meet your God, }
{ For to His throne you'll have to go; Prepare to meet your God. }

2 Lord, cleanse my heart and make me
pure,
To stand before Thy throne,
My pride, and self, and temper cure,
To stand before Thy throne.

3 Why all is in the hands of God.
If death should shake this frame

I'll watch the path the Saviour
trod,
'Till death shall shake this frame.

4 My comrades, fight with all your
might,
Soon death shall shake this frame,
We'll live for God and do what's
right,
Till death shall take this frame,

100 Jesus Paid it All.

1 I hear the Saviour say,
"Thy strength indeed is small:
Child of weakness, watch and pray,
Find in me thine all in all."

CHO. Jesus paid it all:
All to Him I owe;
Sin had left a crimson stain;
He wash'd it white as snow.

2 O Lord, at last I find
Thy power, and Thine alone,

Can change this heart of mine,
And make it all Thine own.

3 Then down beneath the cross
I lay my sin-sick soul;
Nothing I bring but dross,
Thy grace must make me whole.

4 I now in Christ abide;
In Him is perfect rest;
Close sheltered in His side,
I am divinely blest.

81

101   I Will.

Changed by E. L. K.

1. Once more, my soul, thy Saviour, thro' the Word, Is offered full and free ;
2.   By grace I will Thy mercy now receive, Thy love my heart hath won ;
3. Thou knowest, Lord, how ver-y weak I am, And how I fear to stray :
4. And now, O Lord, give all with us to-day The grace to join our song ;
5.   To all who came, when Thou wast here below, And said, "O Lord, wilt Thou ?"

And now, O Lord, I must, I must decide : Shall I ac-cept of Thee?
On Thee, O Christ, I will, I will believe, And trust in Thee a - lone!
For strength to serve I look to Thee a-lone, The strength Thou must supply !
And from the heart, to gladly with us say :" I will to Christ belong !"
To them, "I will !" was ever Thy re-ply : We rest up - on it now.

CHORUS.

I will,   I will,   I will, God helping me, I will be Thine, O

I will,   I will,

Lord : Thy precious blood was shed to purchase me, I will be Thine, O Lord.

82

102 Where the Sun Never Sets.

Arr. by E. L. K. and W. P.

1. There's a cit - y that looks on the Valley of Death, And its glories can nev-er be
2. There the King and Redeemer, the Lord whom we love, All the faithful with rapture be-
3. Every soul we have led to the foot of the Cross, Every Lamb we have brought to the

told; Where the sun never sets and the leaves never fade, In that beautiful City of Gold.
hold, There the righteous forever shall shine as the stars, In that beautiful City of Gold.
fold, Shall be kept as bright jewels our crowns to adorn, In that beautiful City of Gold.

CHORUS.

Where the sun nev-er sets and the leaves nev - er

When the sun nev-er sets and the leaves

fade, And the eyes of the faith - ful their

nev - er fade,

Sav - iour behold, In that beauti - ful Cit-y of Gold.

83

103 All My Heart I Give Thee.

Arr. by E. L. K. and W. P.

1. Je-sus, precious Saviour, Thou has saved my soul From sin's foul cor-
2. From the lowly man-ger, I will follow Thee, In the des-ert
3. In the toils and conflicts, faithful I will be, All things I will

rup -tion, Made me fully whole; Ev'ry hour I'll serve Thee whate'er may be-
and the strife near Thee will I be, E'en the sufferings of the cross I will gladly
gladly bear, they'll be good for me, Live a saviour of mankind, slaves of sin to

fall, Till! in heav'n I crown Thee, King and Lord of all.
bear, If with Thee in heav - en I a crown may wear.
bring, Give me ho - ly cour - age, might-y, might-y King.

Chorus.

All my heart I give Thee, Day by day, come what may,

All my life I give Thee, Thine may it ev - er be!

4 Precious souls are dying, nerve me for the fight,
Help me spread the glorious news, liberty and light;
Fiercer grows the contest now, Satan's pow'r shall fall;
Till on earth I'll crown Thee, glorious Lord of all!

5 When the fight is over, gladly I will stand,
To receive the crown of life from my Saviour's hand.
Then with heavenly ecstacy at Thy feet I'll fall,
And with blood-washed millions, crown Thee Lord of all!

104 Take all my Sins Away.

MARECHALE BOOTH. MARECHALE BOOTH.

1. Oh, spotless Lamb, I come to Thee, No long-er can I from Thee stay,
2. My hungry soul cries out for Thee, Come, and forever seal my breast;
3. Wea-ry I am of in-bred sin, Oh, wilt Thou not my soul release?
4. I plunge beneath Thy precious blood, My hand in faith takes hold on Thee;

S. FINE.

Break ev - 'ry chain, now set me free, Take all my sins a - way.
To Thy dear arms at last I flee, There on - ly can I rest.
En - ter and speak me pure with - in, Give me Thy per-fect peace.
Thy prom-is - es just now I claim, Thou art e-nough for me.

D.s. *My precious Sav-iour, full of love, Take all my sins a - way,*

CHORUS. D. S.

Take all my sins a - way, Take all my sins a - way.

105 All for Jesus.

1 All for Jesus, all for Jesus,
   All my being's ransomed powers,
   All my tho'ts and words and doings,
   All my days and all my hours.

CHORUS.

‖: All for Jesus, all for Jesus,
   All my days and all my hours. :‖

2 Let my hands perform His bidding,
   Let my feet move in His ways,
   Let my eyes see Jesus only,
   Let my lips speak forth His praise.

‖: All for Jesus, all for Jesus,
   Let my lips speak forth His praise. :‖

3 Since my eyes were fixed on Jesus,
   I've lost sight of all beside,
   So enchained my spirit's vision,
   Looking at the crucified.

‖: All for Jesus, all for Jesus,
   All for Jesus crucified. : ‖

4 Oh, what wonder how amazing,
   Jesus—glorious king of kings,
   Deigns to call me His beloved,
   Lets me rest beneath His wings.

‖: All for Jesus, all for Jesus,
   Resting now beneath His wings. :‖

Draw Me Nearer.

"Let us draw near with a true heart." — Heb. 10: 22.

FANNY J. CROSBY.   W. H. DOANE.

1. I am Thine, O Lord, I have heard Thy voice, And it told Thy love to me;
2. Consecrate me now to Thy service, Lord, By the pow'r of grace di - vine;
3. O the pure delight of a single hour That before Thy throne I spend,
4. There are depths of love, That I can-not know Till I cross the narrow sea,

But I long to rise in the arms of faith, And be closer drawn to Thee.
Let my soul look up with a steadfast hope, And my will be lost in Thine.
When I kneel in pray'r, And with Thee, my God, I commune as friend with friend.
There are heights of joy, that I may not reach Till I rest in peace with Thee.

REFRAIN.

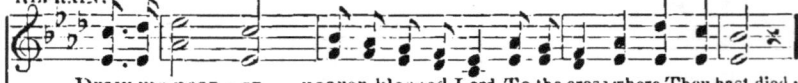

Draw me near - er, nearer, blessed Lord, To the cross where Thou hast died;

nearer, nearer,

Draw me nearer, near-er, nearer blessed Lord, To Thy precious, bleeding side.

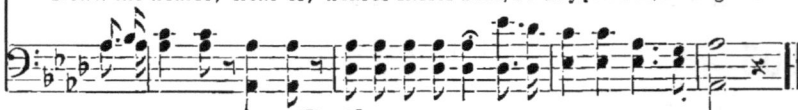

107 Gethsemane.

1 Dark was the hour, Gethsemane,
  When thro' thy walks was heard
The lowly man of Galilee
  Still pleading with the Lord.

CHORUS.

Down in the Garden
  Hear that mournful sound,
There behold your Saviour weeping,
  Praying on the cold, damp ground.

2 Alone in sorrow see Him bow,
  As all our griefs He bears,
Not words can tell His anguish now,
  But sweat, and blood, and tears.

3 There prostrate on the earth He lies,
  God's well beloved Son,
But still the fainting sufferer cries,
  Father, Thy will be done.

4 For me He prays, I hear Him pray,
  He will my soul receive,
Now, Jesus take my sins away,
  Now, Jesus, I believe.

5 Can I forget the tears and blood,
  Which there He shed for me,
They flow a constant cleansing
  flood,
  Abundant, rich, and free.

Consecration.

1 Chr. 29: 5.

FRANCES RIDLEY HAVERGAL.

1. Take my life and let it be   Con - se - cra-ted, Lord, to Thee;
2. Take my feet and let them be   Swift and beau-ti-ful for Thee;
3. Take my lips and let them be   Filled with messages from Thee;
4. Take my moments and my days,   Let them flow in end-less praise;
5. Take my will and make it Thine,   It shall be no long - er mine;
6. Take my love—my Lord, I pour   At Thy feet its treasure-store;

Take my hands and let them move   At the im-pulse of Thy love.
Take my voice and let me sing   Al-ways—on-ly—for my King.
Take my sil - ver and my gold,   Not a mite would I withhold.
Take my in - tel-lect and use   Ev'ry pow'r as Thou shalt choose.
Take my heart, it is Thine own,   It shall be Thy roy-al throne.
Take my-self, and I will be   Ev - er, on - ly, all for Thee.

CHORUS.

Wash me in the Saviour's precious blood,
           the precious blood,
Cleanse me in its pur-i-fy-ing flood,
           the healing flood,
Lord, I give to Thee my

life and all to be, Thine, henceforth, e - ter - nal - ly.

109 The Rock that is Higher.

E. JOHNSON. W. G. FISCHER.

1. Oh, sometimes the shadows are deep, And rough seems the path to the goal, And
2. Oh, sometimes how long seems the day, And sometimes how hea-vy my feet; But
3. Oh, near to the Rock let me keep, Or bless-ings, or sorrows pre-vail; Or

sorrows how oft-en they sweep Like tempests down o-ver the soul.
toil-ing in life's dusty way, The Rock's blessed shadow, how sweet!
climbing, the mountain way steep, Or walking the shadow-y vale.

CHORUS.

O, then to the Rock let me fly, let me fly, To the

Rock that is high-er than I: Oh, then, to the Rock let me
is high - er than I,

is high-er than I,

fly, let me fly, To the Rock that is high-er than I.

There is a Fountain.

1. There is a fountain filled with blood Drawn from our Saviour's veins, And sin-ners plunged beneath the flood, Lose all their guil-ty stains.

Chorus.

I do believe, I now believe, That Jesus died for me, That on the cross. He shed His blood, From sin to set me free.

2 The dying thief rejoiced to see
  That fountain in his day,
And there have I,though vile as he,
  Washed all my sins away.

3 E'er since by faith I saw the stream
  Thy flowing wounds supply,

Redeeming love has been my theme,
  And shall be till I die.

4 Then, in a nobler, sweeter song,
  I'll sing Thy power to save;
When this poor lisping, stamm'ring
  Lies silent in the grave. [tongue

111 Come to Jesus.

1. Come to Je - sus, Come to Je - sus, Come to Je - sus, just now;

Just now come to Je - sus, Come to Je - sus, just now.

2 He will save you.	7 Call upon Him.	12 I do trust Him.
3 Oh, believe Him.	8 He'll forgive you.	13 Jesus save me.
4 He is able.	9 Only trust Him.	14 I love Jesus.
5 He is willing.	10 Jesus loves you.	15 Hallelujah, Amen.
6 He'll receive you.	11 Don't reject Him.	

112 Welcome, Wanderer, Welcome.

Tune :— " WELCOME, WANDERER, WELCOME."

1 In a land of strangers,
　Whither art thou gone;
Hear a sweet voice calling,
　My son, my son.
　　CHORUS.
Welcome, wanderer, welcome,
Welcome back to home;
Thou hast wandered far away,
Come home, come home.

2 From a land of hunger,
　Fainted, famished, lone,

Come in love and gladness,
　My son, my son.

3 See the well-spread table,
　Unforgotten one;
Here is rest and plenty,
　My son, my son.

4 Thou art homeless, friendless,
　Helpless and undone:
Mine is love unchanging,
　My son, my son.

113 Are You Coming Home?

1 Are you coming home, ye wander-
　Whom Jesus died to win, 　[ers,
All footsore, lame, and weary,
　Your garments stained with sin?
Will you seek the blood of Jesus
　To wash your garments white?
Will you trust His precious prom-
　ise,
Are you coming home to-night?
　　CHORUS.
‖: Are you coming home to-night, :‖
　Are you coming home to Jesus,
Out of darkness into light?
‖: Are you coming home to-night, :‖
　To your loving, heavenly Father,
Are you coming home to-night?

2 Are you coming home, ye guilty,
　Who bear the load of sin?
Outside you've long been standing,
　Come now and venture in;
Will you heed the Saviour's prom-
　ise,
　And dare to trust Him quite?
" Come unto Me," saith Jesus,
　Are you coming home to-night?

3 Are you coming home, ye lost ones,
　Behold your Lord doth wait;
Come, then, no longer linger,
　Come ere it be too late;
Will you come and let Him save
　you?
Oh, trust His love and might;
Will you come, He is calling,
　Are you coming home to-night?

90

114 Room for Thee.

"There was no room for them in the inn."— Luke 2: 7.

EMILY S. ELLIOTT.   IRA D. SANKEY.

1. Thou didst leave Thy throne, and Thy kingly crown, When Thou camest to earth for
2. Heav'n's arch - es rang when the angels sang Of Thy birth and Thy royal de-
3. Foxes found their rest, and the birds had their nests, In the shade of the cedar
4. Thou camest, O Lord, with Thy living word, That should set Thy peo-ple
5. Heav'n's arches shall ring, and its choirs shall sing, At Thy coming to vic-to-

me; But in Bethlehem's home there was found no room, For Thy holy nativ - i - ty.
cree: But in low - ly birth didst Thou come to earth, And in greatest humil - i - ty.
tree; But Thy couch was the sod, O Thou Son of God, In the deserts of Gal - i-lee.
free; But with mocking and scorn and with crown of thorn Did they bear Thee to Calvary.
ry, Thou wilt call me home, saying "yet there is room, There is room at My side for thee."

REFRAIN.

Oh, come to my heart, Lord Je-sus! There is room in my heart for Thee.

Oh, come to my heart, Lord Je-sus, Come! there is room in my heart for Thee.

115   Jesus of Nazareth Passeth By.

1 What means this eager, anxious
   throng,
 Which moves with busy haste along,
 These wondrous gatherings day by
   day?   [tion, pray?
 What means this strange commo-
 ‖ : In accents hushed the throng
   reply
 " Jesus of Nazareth passeth by." : ‖

2 Who is this Jesus? Why should He
 The city move so mightily?

A passing stranger, has He skill
To move the multitude at will?
‖ : Again the stirring notes reply :
" Jesus of Nazareth passeth by." : ‖

3 Ho! all ye heavy laden, come :
 Here's pardon, comfort, rest and
   home,
 Ye wand'rers from a Father's face,
 Return, accept His proffered grace,
 ‖ : Ye tempted ones, there's refuge
   nigh—
 " Jesus of Nazareth passeth by !" : ‖

116 Only Trust Him.

J. H. S.   Rev. J. H. STOCKTON.

1. Come, ev-'ry soul by sin oppress'd, There's mercy with the Lord : And He will surely give you rest, by trusting in His word.

CHORUS.

On - ly trust Him, on-ly trust Him, On-ly trust Him now ; He will save you, He will save you, He will save you now.

2 For Jesus shed His precious blood,
  Rich blessings to bestow;
Plunge now into the crimson flood
  That washes white as snow.

3 Yes, Jesus is the truth, the way
  That leads you into rest;
Believe in Him without delay
  And you are fully blest.

4 O Jesus, blessed Jesus, dear,
  I'm coming now to Thee; [clear,
Since Thou hast made the way so
  And full salvation free.

5 Come, then, and join this holy band
  And on to glory go;
To dwell in that celestial land,
  Where joys immortal flow.

117 I Know that My Redeemer Lives.

1 I know that my Redeemer lives
  And ever prays for me;
A token of His love He gives—
  A pledge of liberty.

CHORUS.
The cleansing stream, I see, I see!
  I trust, and oh, it cleanseth me!
Oh, praise the Lord, it cleanseth me;
  It cleanseth me—yes, cleanseth me.

2 I find Him lifting up my head;
  He brings salvation near;

His presence makes me free indeed
  And He will soon appear.

3 When God is mine and I am His,
  Of paradise possessed,
I taste unutterable bliss
  And everlasting rest.

4 Thou onlyknow'st, who didst obtain
  And die to make it known,
The great salvation now explain,
  And perfect us in one.

C. WESLEY.

118   I Am Listening.

"It is the voice of my beloved that knocketh, saying, Open to me."—Cant. 5: 2.

W. S. MARSHALL.   W. S. MARSHALL.

1. Do you hear the Sav-iour call - ing, By the wooings of His
2. By His Spir - it He is woo-ing, Soft - ly drawing us to
3. By the Word of truth He's speaking, To the wand'ring, erring
4. In His Prov - i - den - tial deal- ings, E - ven in His stern de-

voice? Do you hear the accents falling? Will you make the precious choice?
Him, Thro' the day and night pursuing, With His gentle voice to win.
ones; List! the voice the stillness breaking! Hear the sweet and solemn tones!
crees, In the loudest thunders pealing, Or the murm'ring of the breeze,

REFRAIN.

I am list'ning, Oh, I'm list-'ning, Just to hear the accents

Repeat softly.

fall; I am list'ning, Oh, I'm list'ning, To the Saviour's loving call.

93

Jesus Now is Passing By.

Luke 18: 37.

Words and music by R. E. HUDSON.

1. Come, wea-ry sinner, to the cross; The Saviour bids you come; Come,
2. Oh! why de-lay your long return? The Spirit gen-tly pleads; Come
3. He waits to fill your soul with joy, And all your sins forgive; His

trust-ing in His precious blood; Wait not there still is room.
to the cross whereon for you The dy-ing Saviour bleeds.
love for you no tongue can tell; Oh! trust His grace and live!

CHORUS.

{ Some poor soul is draw-ing nigh, Drawing nigh, drawing nigh.
He has heard that in-most sigh, In-most sigh, inmost sigh.

Some poor soul is drawing nigh, Christ is here to meet him. }
God has heard that humble sigh, Do come out and meet him. }

The Glorious Fountain.

"In that day there shall be a fountain opened, for sin and uncleanness."—Zech. 13: 1.

COWPER.   T. C. O'KANE.

1. { There is a foun-tain filled with blood, filled with blood, filled with blood, There
   { And sinners plunged beneath that flood, Beneath that flood, be-neath that flood, And

is a fountain filled with blood Drawn from Im-man-uel's veins; }
sinners plunged beneath that flood Lose all their guil - ty stains. }

CHORUS.

Oh, glo - ri - ous foun - tain! Here will I stay,

And in Thee ev - er Wash my sins a - way!

2 The dying thief rejoiced to see
   That fountain in his day;
   And there may I, though vile as he,
   Wash all my sins away.

3 Thou dying Lamb, Thy precious
        blood
   Shall never lose its power,
   Till all the ransomed Church of God
   Are saved, to sin no more.

4 E'er since, by faith, I saw the stream
   Thy flowing wounds supply,
   Redeeming love has been my theme,
   And shall be till I die.

5 Then in a nobler, sweeter song
   I'll sing Thy power to save,
   When this poor lisping, stammering
        tongue,
   Lies silent in the grave.

121 Diamonds in the Rough.

C. P. BAKER.   Changed by E. L. K.

1. The human wrecks are many, they lay a-long the shore, They seem to be so
2. Ma-ny are the aching hearts,—we find them everywhere, Who pray for sons and
3. Now others, whom we'll not forget, are victims of the foe, Have lost good homes, and

helpless, as the breakers 'gainst them roar. Some peo-ple pass them by the way; I
husbands, to leave the tempter's snare;   The money when 'tis all used up the
dwell in shame, their cups are filled with woe, Their hearts do bleed when they reflect, Oh

think it 's rath-er tough. But speak kind words and you will find they're diamonds in the rough.
world gives them a   cuff, To jail or poorhouse they must go, those diamonds in the rough.
it is sad e - nough, Oh, comrades, let us try and dig those diamonds in the rough.

CHORUS.

Christian crusaders, 'tis for you to give a helping hand; Good people all will

cheer you on because the work is grand; There's many, it is sad to say, that

Diamonds in the Rough. Concluded.

gives us a re-buff, While digging in the sands of time for diamonds in the rough.

122 At the Cross.

CHAS. WESLEY.

1. O! how hap - py are they Who the Sav - iour o - bey, And have
2. That sweet comfort was mine When the fa - vor di - vine I re-
3. 'Twas a heav - en be - low, my Re - deem - er to know, The an-
4. Je - sus all the day long Was my joy and my song: O that

REF. At the cross, at the cross, Where I first saw the light, And the

laid up their treasure a-bove; Tongue can nev er ex-press the sweet
ceived thro' the blood of the Lamb; When my heart first believed, What a
gels could do noth - ing more Than fall at His feet, And the
all His sal - va - tion might see! He hath loved me, I cried, He hath

bur-den of my heart roll'd a - way, It was there by faith I re-

com - fort and peace Of a soul in its ear - li - est love.
joy I received, What a heav - en in Je - sus' name.
sto - ry re-peat, And the lov - er of sinners a - dore.
suf-fered and died, To re-deem ev - en reb-els like me.

ceived my sight, And now I am hap - py night and day.

97

123 Let me Die.

Arr. by C. P. Baker.

1. O God, my heart doth long for Thee; Let me die:
2. My friends may say "I'll ruin-ed be;" If I die:
3. Oh, I must die to scoffs and jeers, Let me die:

Now set my soul at lib - er - ty, Let me die;
If I leave all and fol - low Thee, But I'll die,
I must be freed from slav - ish fears, Let me die,

Die to the trif - ling things of earth, They're now to me of
Their ar - gu - ments will nev - er weigh, Nor stand the try - ing
So dead that no de - sire shall rise To ap - pear good, or

lit - tle worth, My Saviour calls, I'm go-ing forth; Let me die.
judgment day; Help me to cast them all a - way; Let me die.
great, or wise, In a - ny but my Saviour's eyes; Let me die.

4 If Christ would live and reign in me
  I must die;
  Like Him I crucified must be;
  I must die. [groans,
  Lord, drive the nails nor heed the
  My flesh may writhe and make its
  moans,
  But this the way, and this alone;
  I must die.

5 When I am dead, then, Lord, to Thee
  I shall live;
  My time, my strength, my all to Thee
  Will I give.
  O may the Son now make me free!
  Here, Lord I give my all to Thee,
  For Thine and eternity
  I will live.

Belmont.

DR. BONAR. FROM MOZART.

1. I heard the voice of Je - sus say, "Come un - to Me and rest;
   I came to Je - sus as I was, Wea-ry and worn and sad,

Lay down, thou weary one, lay down Thy head up - on My breast."
I found in Him a rest - ing place, And He has made me glad.

CHORUS.

Come away, come away,
   Come away, to Jesus;
Come away, come away home,
   For Jesus waits to save you.

2 I heard the voice of Jesus say,
   " Behold, I freely give
The living water; thirsty one,
   Stoop down, and drink, and live."
I came to Jesus, and I drank
   Of that life-giving stream:

My thirst was quenched, my soul
   revived,
And now I live in Him.

3 I heard the voice of Jesus say,
   " I am this dark world's Light;
Look unto Me, thy morn shall rise,
   And all thy day be bright."
I looked to Jesus, and I found
   In Him my Star, my Sun;
And in that Light of life I'll walk
   Till traveling days are done.

View the Land.

I never shall forget the day, View the land, view the land When Jesus wash'd my sins away;

FULL CHORUS.

View the heav'nly land. A-way ov-er Jordan, View the land, view the land; Away over

Jor-dan To view the heav'nly land.

2 I once was blind, but now I see;
   I once was bound, but now am free.

3 A little longer here below,
   Then home to glory I shall go.

126 On the happy Golden Shore.

TUNE. "*Meet me there.*" KEY OF E FLAT.

1 On the happy golden shore,
　Where the faithful part no more,
　When the storms of life are o'er,
　　Meet me there.
　Where the night dissolves away,
　Into pure and perfect day,
　I'm going home to stay,
　　Meet me there.

CHORUS.

Meet me there.　meet me there.
Where the tree of life is blooming,
　Meet me there.
When the storms of life are o'er,
On the golden happy shore,
Where the faithful part no more,
　Meet me there.

2 Here our fondest hopes are vain,
　Dearest links are rent in twain,
　But in heaven no throb of pain,
　　Meet me there.
　By the river sparkling bright,
　In the city of delight,
　Where our faith is lost in sight,
　　Meet me there.

3 Where the harps of angels ring,
　And the blest forever sing
　In the palace of the King,
　　Meet me there.
　Where in sweet communion blend,
　Heart with heart, and friend with
　　friend,
　In the world that ne'er shall end,
　　Meet me there.

127 Are you washed?

1 Have you been to Jesus for the
　cleansing power?
　Are you washed in the blood of
　the Lamb?
　Are you fully trusting in His grace
　this hour?
　Are you washed in the blood of
　the Lamb?

CHO.—Are you washed in the blood,
　　In the soul-cleansing blood
　　of the Lamb?
　　Are your garments spotless?
　　Are they white as snow?
　　Are you washed in the blood
　　of the Lamb?

2 Are you walking daily by the
　Saviour's side?
　Are you washed in the blood of
　the Lamb?
　Do you rest each moment in the
　crucified?
　Are you washed in the blood of
　the Lamb?

3 When the Bridegroom cometh will
　your robes be white,
　Pure and white in the blood of
　the Lamb?
　Will your soul be ready for the
　mansions bright?
　And be washed in the blood of
　the Lamb?

4 Lay aside the garments that are
　stained with sin,
　And be washed in the blood of
　the Lamb;
　There's a fountain flowing for the
　soul unclean—
　O be washed in the blood of the
　Lamb!

128 Blessed be the Name of the Lord!

1 Oh, sinner, come to Jesus, and give
　your heart to Him;
　Blessed be the name of the Lord!
　And He will make you holy, and
　save you from all sin;
　Blessed be the name of the Lord!

CHORUS.

When the stars of the elements are
　falling,
And the moon shall be turned into
　blood,
And the children of the Lord, re-
　turning home to God,
　Blessed be the name of the Lord!

2 And when the Lord does call us, to
　cross dark Jordan's tide,
　Blessed be the name of the Lord!
　I'm sure that He will help us, and
　be close by our side,
　Blessed be the name of the Lord!

3 Then our mission will be over, and
　all our work be done;
　Blessed be the name of the Lord!
　We'll bind our sheaves together,
　and shout the harvest home;
　Blessed be the name of the Lord!

SECOND CHORUS.

Blessed be the name, blessed be
　the name,
Blessed be the name of the Lord!
Oh, blessed be the name, blessed
　be the name,
Blessed be the name of the Lord!

129 Just as I am.

1 Just as I am — without one plea,
But that Thy blood was shed for
me, [Thee,
And that Thou bidst me come to
O Lamb of God, I come!

2 Just as I am — and waiting not
To rid my soul of one dark blot,—
To Thee whose blood can cleanse
each spot
O Lamb of God, I come!

3 Just as I am—though toss'd about,
With many a conflict, many a doubt,
Fightings within and fears without,
O Lamb of God, I come!

4 Just as I am—poor, wretched, blind;
Sight, riches, healing of the mind,
Yea, all I need, in Thee to find,
O Lamb of God, I come!

5 Just as I am — Thou wilt receive,
Wilt welcome, pardon, cleanse, re-
lieve,
Because Thy promise I believe,
O Lamb of God, I come!

6 Just as I am — Thy love I own,
Has broken every barrier down:
Now to be Thine, yea, Thine alone,
O Lamb of God, I come!

130 I am Trusting.

1 All my doubts I give to Jesus —
I've His gracious promise heard—
I " shall never be confounded;"
I am trusting in that word.

CHORUS.
I am trusting, fully trusting;
Only trusting in His word.

2 All my sin I lay on Jesus,
He doth wash me in His blood;

He doth keep me pure and holy;
He will bring me home to God.

3 All my fears I give to Jesus —
Rests my weary soul on Him —
Though my way be hid in darkness,
Never can His light grow dim.

4 All my joys I give to Jesus,
He is all I want of bliss;
He of all the world is master;
He has all I need in this.

5 All I am I give to Jesus —
All my body, all my soul,
All I have, and all I hope for,
While eternal ages roll.

131 Papa, Come this Way.

1 A little childish voice is stilled,
Two little lily white hands are
crossed,
Two little eyes forever closed;
The sound of pattering feet is
lost.
A little form from out our home
Was borne by loving hands away,
But still I seem to hear a voice
Within my heart, it says each day:

CHORUS.
Papa, come this way, papa, come
this way,
A little voice calls from that shore,
Papa, come this way.

2 I'm sure my darling is at rest
Within Thy tender Shepherd's
fold,
He took her from this sinful world,
He shields her from its blast and
cold.
But how I miss the loving kiss,
And oh! my longing heart is sore;
Then comes that little pleading
voice,
It gently whispers o'er and o'er:

3 Where'er I go, that voice I hear,
As though my darling could not
Until I gave my heart to Him [rest,
Who died to save and make me
And so it echoes in my heart. [blest.
And through the chambers of my
soul:
I'll not resist that pleading voice,
I'll go to Jesus and be whole.

132 Pass Me Not.

1 Pass me not, O gentle Saviour,
Hear my humble cry;
While on others Thou art smiling,
Do not pass me by.

CHORUS.

Saviour, Saviour, hear my humble cry;
While on others Thou art calling,
Do not pass me by.

2 Let me at a throne of mercy
Find a sweet relief,
Kneeling there in deep contrition,
Help my unbelief.

3 Trusting only in Thy merit,
Would I seek Thy face;
Heal my wounded, broken spirit,
Save me by Thy grace.

4 Thou the Spring of all my comfort,
More than life to me,
Whom have I on earth beside Thee?
Whom in heaven but Thee?

133 I Hear Thy Welcome Voice.

L. HARTSOUGH.

1 I hear Thy welcome voice,
That calls me, Lord, to Thee,
For cleansing in Thy precious
That flowed on Calvary. [blood,

CHORUS.
I am coming, Lord,
Coming now to Thee!
Wash me, cleanse me in the blood
That flowed on Calvary.

2 'Tis Jesus calls me on
To perfect faith and love, [trust,
To perfect hope, and peace, and
For earth and heaven above.

3 And He the witness gives
To loyal hearts and free,
That every promise is fulfilled,
If faith but brings the plea.

4 All hail, atoning blood!
All hail, redeeming grace! [Lord,
All hail, the gift of Christ our
Our Strength and Righteousness!

134 A Heart of Praise.

1 O for a heart to praise my God,
A heart from sin set free,
A heart that always feels the blood
So freely spilt for me!

2 A heart resigned, submissive, meek,
My great Redeemer's throne;
Where only Christ is heard to speak,
Where Jesus reigns alone.

3 An humble, lowly, contrite heart,
Believing, true and clean : [part
Which neither life nor death can
From Him that dwells within.

4 A heart in every thought renewed,
And full of love Divine;
Perfect and right, and pure and
A copy, Lord, of Thine. [good,

5 Thy nature, gracious Lord, impart;
Come quickly from above ; [heart,
Write Thy new name upon my
Thy new, best name of Love.

135 Precious Jesus.

1 Precious Jesus, oh! to love Thee,
Oh! to know that Thou art mine;
Jesus, all my heart I give Thee,
If Thou wilt but make it Thine.
Jesus, Jesus, precious Jesus,
Thou art all in all to me.

2 Take my warmest, best affections,
Take my memory, mind and will;
Then, with all Thy loving spirit,
All my emptied nature fill.

3 Bold I touch Thy sacred garment,
Fearless stretch my eager hand;
Virtue, like a healing fountain,
Freely flows at love's command.

4 Oh, how precious, dear Redeemer,
Is the love that fills my soul!
It is done, the word is spoken,
Be thou every whit made whole.

5 Lo! a new creation dawning;
Lo! I rise to life divine;
In my soul an Easter morning;
I am Christ's and Christ is mine!

136 Ring the Bells.

Rev. W. O. CUSHING. (G. II. 19.)

1 Ring the bells of heaven! there is
    joy to-day, [wild;
For a soul returning from the
See! the Father meets him out up-
    on the way, [ing child.
Welcoming His weary, wander-

CHORUS.

Glory! glory! how the angels sing;
Glory! glory! how the loud harps
    ring; [mighty sea,
'T is the ransom'd army, like a
Pealing forth the anthem of the free.

2 Ring the bells of heaven! there is
    joy to-day, [ciled:
For the wanderer now is recon-
Yes, a soul is rescued from his sin-
    ful way, [child.
And is born anew a ransomed

3 Ring the bells of heaven! spread
    the feast to-day, [ant strain!
Angels swell the glad triumph-
Tell the joyous tidings! bear it far
    away,
For a precious soul is born again.

137 On the Cross of Calvary.

1 On the cross of Calvary,
  Jesus suffered for you and me,
There He shed His precious blood
    That from sin we might be free.
Oh the precious blood doth flow,
And it washes white as snow,
It was for me that Jesus suffered,
  On the cross of Calvary.

CHORUS.

On Calvary, on Calvary,
It was for me that Jesus suffered,
On the Cross of Calvary.

2 Oh, 't was love, 't was wondrous
    love,
  Brought me down at Jesus' feet,
Oh, such wondrous dying love,
  Asks a sacrifice complete.
Here I give myself to Thee,
Soul and body Thine to be;
It was for me that Jesus suffered,
  On the cross of Calvary.

3 Clouds and darkness veil'd the sky
  When the Lord was crucified;
" It is finished," was His cry,
  And he bowed His head and died.
It is finished, it is finished,
All the world may now go free,
It was for me that Jesus suffered,
  On the cross of Calvary.

138 The Storms will be Over.

1 We are out on the ocean sailing,
  Homeward bound we sweetly
    glide;
We are out on the ocean sailing,
  To our home beyond the tide.

CHORUS.

All the storms will soon be over,
Then we 'll anchor in the harbor;
We are out on the ocean sailing,
To our home beyond the tide.

2 Millions now are safely landed
  Over on the golden shore;
Millions more are on their journey,
  Yet there 's room for millions
    more.

3 Come on board and ship for glory;
  Be in haste, make up your mind,
For our vessel 's weighing anchor,
  You will soon be left behind.

4 You have kindred over yonder,
  On that bright and happy shore;
By-and-by we 'll swell the number,
  When the toils of life are o'er.

5 Spread your sails while heavenly
    breezes
  Swiftly waft our vessels on;
All on board are loudly singing;
  Free salvation is the song.

6 When we all are safely anchored
  Over on the shining shore,
We will march about the city,
  And we 'll sing for evermore.

139 Every Day and Hour.

F. J. CROSBY. (G. II. 48.)

1 Saviour, more than life to me,
  I am clinging, clinging close to
    Thee!
Let Thy precious blood applied,
Keep me ever, ever near Thy side.

CHORUS.

Every day, every hour,
Let me feel Thy cleansing power;
May Thy tender love to me [Thee.
Bind me closer, closer, Lord, to

2 Through this changing world be-
    low,
Lead me gently, gently as I go;
Trusting Thee, I cannot stray,
I can never, never lose my way.

3 Let me love Thee more and more,
  Till this fleeting, fleeting life is o'er;
Till my soul is lost in love
In a brighter, brighter world above.

140 Don't Go near the Bar-Room.

TUNE:—"*Just before the Battle.*"
KEY OF B-FLAT.

1 Don't go near the bar-room, brother,
   Listen to a sister's prayer,
   Do not yield to its temptation, —
   Sin and death are lurking there.
   Do not heed the gilded palace,
   'T is a mask the tempter wears,
   For deep destruction lurks beneath
   it,
   And will meet you unawares.

CHORUS.

Dearest brother, will you never
From the luring wine abstain,
O by the love you bear me, brother,
Break, O break the demon's chain.

2 Don't go near the bar-room, brother,
   Shun it as an evil place;
   It will bring you desolation, —
   Cover you with deep disgrace.
   Friends and kindred all around you,
   ' Counsel you to pass it by :
   The pleadings of your darling sister
   Strengthen you once more to try.

3 Don't go near the bar-room brother,
   Touch not, taste not of the wine,
   There is poison in its contact, —
   Do not worship at its shrine.
   Join the grand teetotal army,
   Shun the bar-room and the cup,
   Then in strong love we 'll work to-
   gether,
   Till the demon shall give up.

141 A Shelter in the time of Storm.

1 The Lord's our Rock, in Him we
   hide,
   A shelter in the time of storm,
   Secure whatever ill betide,
   A shelter in the time of storm.

CHORUS.

Oh, Jesus is a rock in a weary land,
A weary land, a weary land,
Oh, Jesus is a rock in a weary land,
A shelter in the time of storm.

2 A shade by day, defence by night,
   No fears alarm, no foes affright.

3 The raging storms may round us
   beat,
   We'll never leave our safe retreat,

4 O Rock divine, O Refuge dear,
   Be Thou our helper ever near.

142 A Plea to Sinners.

TUNE:—"*My Old Kentucky Home.*"

1 The sun shines bright
   In my once sin-stricken home,
   We 're happy and merry to-day;
   I've joined hands with God,
   And from Him I'll never roam. [day.
   For His love makes me happy all the

CHORUS.

Weep no more, poor sinner,
Weep no more— but pray;
Give Jesus your heart
And accept His precious Word,
Then, like me, you'll be happy all
   the day.

2 If your days go by
   As a cloud upon your heart,
   Your sorrow can all be made light;
   Just accept Him now,
   You'll never want to part,
   But, like me, you'll be happy, gay
   and bright.

3 The Master awaits you;
   Oh, sinner, hear His call;
   Oh, why not accept Him to-night?
   You'll find if you do
   That He 's loving, kind and true;
   Just trust Him and He will set you
   right.

143 The Cross now Covers My Sin.

1 I stand all bewildered with wonder,
   And gaze on the ocean of love,
   And over it waves to my spirit
   Comes peace, like a heavenly dove.

CHORUS.

The cross now covers my sins,
The past is under the blood,
I'm trusting in Jesus for all.
My will is the will of my God.

2 I struggled and wrestled to win it,
   The blessing that setteth me
   free ;   [struggles,
   But when I had ceased from my
   His peace Jesus gave unto me.

3 He laid His hand on me, and healed
   me,   [whole :
   And bade me be every whit
   I touched but the hem of His gar-
   ment,
   And glory came thrilling my soul.

4 The Prince of my Peace is now
   passing,
   The light of His face is on me ;
   But listen, beloved, He speaketh —
   " My peace I will give unto thee."

1 Lord Jesus, I long to be perfectly whole,
I want Thee forever to live in my soul;
Break down every idol, cast out every foe;
Now wash me and I shall be whiter than snow.

CHORUS.

Whiter than snow, yes, whiter than snow,
Now wash me and I shall be whiter than snow.

2 Lord Jesus, let nothing unholy remain;
Apply Thine own blood and remove every stain;
To get this blest washing I all things forego;
Now wash me and I shall be whiter than snow.

3 Lord Jesus, come down from Thy throne in the skies,
And help me to make a complete sacrifice,
I give up myself and whatever I know;
Now wash me and I shall be whiter than snow.

4 Lord Jesus, Thou seest I patiently wait,
Come now and within me a new heart create;
To those who have sought Thee Thou never saidst " No ; "
Now wash me and I shall be whiter than snow.

5 Thy blessing by faith I receive from above,
Oh ! glory ! my soul is made perfect in love:
My prayer has prevailed and this moment I know
The blood is applied — I am whiter than snow.

145   The Wanderer's Return.

TUNE: —*Swanee River.*

1 How many were the years I wandered far from the fold,
How many were the days I squandered way on the mountain cold,
Oh, how the clouds so often gathered, round my pathway dark,
And many were the storms I weathered, ere the shepherd brought me back.

CHORUS.

Wanderer, if you knew the glory
Fills this heart of mine,
How gladly you would hear my story,
And bow at mercy's shrine.

2 How many times I heard Him calling, but my heart was cold,
And often while the tears were falling, heard I the story told,
How on the cross He groaned and suffered for my guilt and sin,
And when to Him my heart I offered, gladly He took me in.

3 Since then how sweet has been life's toiling, close by his side,
He tells me with His dear face smiling, "I will with you abide."
Though many foes may be around me, He is with me still,
And though the tossing waves surround me, He will say," Peace, be still."

4 Oh precious soul, the Saviour's calling, why longer roam,
Earth cannot satisfy thy longing, Jesus will lead thee home.
Kneel at the cross, He bore thy sorrow, He will now forgive.
Oh do not say this time " to-morrow," you may no longer live.

We are in the Service.

Tune:— "RING THE BELLS OF HEAVEN."

1 We are in the service, fighting for the King,
    And we know our sins are all forgiven.
  With our happy comrades we can shout and sing,
    We are on the royal road to heaven.

CHORUS.

  Sing, soldiers, sing, and let the people hear!
  Shout, soldiers, shout, and never, never fear!
  If we keep believing we are sure to win;
  "Blood and Fire" is sure to conquer sin.

2 In the name of Jesus, onward we will go.
    And of free Salvation we will sing;
  Clad in Gospel armor, we will face the foe,
    And the world to Jesus' feet we'll bring.

3 Though our foes be mighty, and the fight severe,
    Trusting in the King we'll march along.
  Jesus is our Leader, we will never fear,
    He can make the weakest soldier strong.

4 Blow the Gospel trumpet, wield the two-edged sword!
    Tell the world that Jesus died to save;
  Forward to the conflict, trusting in the Lord,
    He will make His soldiers bold and brave.

5 Courage, then, my comrades, Jesus is our friend,
    He will lead and guide us in the fight;
  He will keep us faithful to our journey's end,
    If we keep the Gospel armor bright.

147   Begone, Vain World.

1 Begone, vain world, thou hasts no charms for me,
  My captive soul has long been held by thee;
    I listened long to thy vain song,
    And thought thy music sweet,
  And thus my soul lay grovelling at thy feet.

2 What are thy charms, could I command the whole?
  Thy mingled sweets could never feed a soul.
    A nobler prize attracts mine eyes,
    Where trees immortal grow.
  A fruitful land where milk and honey flow.

3 My soul through grace, on wings of faith shall rise
  Towards that dear place where my possession lies;
    That sacred land, at God's right hand,
    My dear Redeemer's throne,
  Where Jesus pleads, and makes my cause His own.

4 Amazing grace! does Jesus plead for me?
  Then sure I am the captive must be free;
    For while He does for sinners plead,
    He's anxious to prevail,
  And I believe His blood can never fail.

5 He signed the deed with His atoning blood,
  And ever lives to make the payment good;
    Should hell, and sin, and law come in,
    To urge a second claim,
  They all retire at mention of His name.

6 Then let me rise and hasten to that day;
  The grace, the song, invite my soul away.
    Fired with that love, my soul above
    Shall join the blissful throng,
  And grace, free grace and glory crown the song.

148   I am Saved.

1 I am saved! I am saved!
  Jesus bids me go free!
I am bought with a price,
  Even me, even me.

CHORUS.

Hallelujah, Hallelujah,
  Hallelujah to my Saviour!
Hallelujah, Hallelujah,
  Hallelujah, Amen.

2 Wondrous love! wondrous love
  Now the gifts I receive;
I have rest in this world;
  I believe! I believe!

3 I am cleansed! I am cleansed!
  I am whiter than snow!
He is mighty to save,
  This I know! this I know!

4 I was weak! I am strong!
  In the power of his might;
And my darkness he's turned
  Into light, into light.

5 Praise the Lord! Praise the Lord!
  All His saints everywhere;
I shall join in that throng
  Over there; over there.

149   Cast thy Bread upon the Waters.

1 Cast thy bread upon the waters,
  Ye who have but scant supply,
Angel eyes will watch above it,
  You shall find it by and by.
He who in his righteous balance,
  Doth each human action weigh,
Will your sacrifice remember,
  Will your loving deeds repay.

2 Cast thy bread upon the waters,
  Poor and weary worn with care,
Often sitting in the shadow,
  Have you not a crumb to spare?
Can you not to those around you,
  Sing some little song of hope,
As you look with longing vision,
  Through faith's mighty telescope?

3 Cast thy bread upon the waters,
  Ye who have abundant store,
It may float on many a billow,
  It may strand on many a shore.

You may think it lost forever,
  Be as sure as God is true,
In this life or in the other,
  It may yet return to you.

4 Cast thy bread upon the waters,
  Far and wide your treasures
    strew,
Scatter it with willing fingers,
  Shout for joy to see it go.
For if you do closely keep it,
  It will surely drag you down,
If you love it more than Jesus,
  It will keep you from your crown.

5 Cast thy bread upon the waters,
  Waft it on with praying breath,
In some distant doubtful movement,
  It may save a soul from death.
When you sleep in solemn silence,
  'Neath the morn or evening dew,
Strangers' hands which you have
    strengthened,
  May strew lilies over you.

150   The Precious Name.

1 Take the Name of Jesus with you,
  Child of sorrow and of woe,
It will joy and comfort give you,
  Take it then where'er you go.

CHORUS.

Precious Name, O how sweet!
Hope of earth and joy of heaven.

2 Take the Name of Jesus ever
  As a shield from every snare;
If temptations round you gather,
  Breathe that Holy Name in
    prayer.

3 Oh! the precious Name of Jesus;
  How it thrills our souls with joy,
When His loving arms receive us,
  And His songs our tongues em-
    ploy!

4 At the Name of Jesus bowing,
  Falling prostrate at His feet,
King of kings in heaven we'll
    crown Him,
  When our journey is complete.

151
Glory to His Name.

1 Down at the Cross where my Saviour died
  Down where for cleansing from sin I cried;
  There to my heart was the blood applied,
  Glory to His name!

· Chorus.

Glory to His name!
Glory to His name!
There to my heart was the blood applied,
Glory to His name!

2 I am so wondrously saved from sin,
  Jesus so sweetly abides within;
  There at the Cross where He took me in,
  Glory to His name!

3 Oh, precious fountain, that saves from sin,
  I am so glad I have entered in;
  There Jesus saves me and keeps me clean,
  Glory to His name!

4 Come to this fountain, so nice and sweet;
  Cast thy poor soul at the Saviour's feet;
  Plunge in to-day and be made complete;
  Glory to His name!

152
Follow! Follow!

1 Down in the valley with my Saviour I would go,
  Where the flowers are blooming and the sweet waters flow;
  Ev'rywhere He leads me I would follow, follow on,
  Walking in His footsteps till the crown be won.

Chorus.

Follow! Follow! I would follow Jesus;
  Anywhere, ev'rywhere, I would follow on!
Follow! Follow! I would follow Jesus;
  Ev'rywhere He leads me I would follow on.

2 Down in the valley with my Saviour I would go,
  Where the the storms are sweeping and the dark waters flow,
  With His hand to lead me I will never, never fear;
  Dangers cannot fright me if my Lord is near.

3 Down in the valley or upon the mountain steep,
  Close beside my Saviour would my soul ever keep;
  He would lead me safely in the path that He has trod,
  Up to where they gather on the hills of God.

108

1 Oh the drunkard may come and the swearer may come,
Backsliders and sinners are all welcome home;
If you will but repent and be washed in the blood
Forever and ever you will dwell with the Lord.

2 Higher than I, higher than I,
Resting on the rock that is higher than I.

3 There are angels hovering round
To carry the tidings home,
Poor sinners are coming home,
And Jesus bids them come.
He shed His blood for you,
He died that you might live,
Oh come to Jesus now,
There's mercy still for you,
He'll take your sins away.

4 Building up the temple, building up the temple,
Building up the temple of the Lord. (Repeat).

5 I'm going home to glory, I'm going home to glory,
I'm going to the mansion that's prepared for you and me;
I'm going home to glory, I'm going home to glory,
We anchor in the harbor by and by.

6 I'm going to live with Jesus, don't you grieve after me,
I don't want you to grieve after me.

7 We're marching on to war,
We are, we are, we are;
We care not what the people think,
Or what they say we are.
We mean to fight for Jesus,
Who did salvation bring;
We're hallelujah soldiers,
And we're going to see the King.

8 The day of victory is coming,
Is coming by and by;
When to the Cross of Calvary,
All nations they will fly.
We're Christian Crusaders, we'll fight until we die,
For the day of victory is coming by and by.

9 By and by we'll see the King,
By and by we'll see the King,
By and by we'll see the King,
And crown Him Lord of all.

10 By the Blood my Saviour shed upon the tree,
He redeemed me, Hallelujah;
By the Blood my Saviour shed upon the tree.
I'm now from sin set free.

11 Oh, the precious blood,
Oh, the precious blood,
The blood that was shed on Calvary,
Oh, the precious blood,
Oh, the precious blood,
The blood that was shed for me.

12 Oh, the precious blood is flowing o'er my heart,
It is cleansing, Hallelujah!
And before its waves my sin and fear depart.
It is flowing o'er my heart.

13 I'm saved, I am, I know I am,
I'm washed in Jesus' blood;
I'm saved, I am, I know I am,
I'm washed in Jesus' blood;
I'm saved, I am, I know I am,
I'm washed in Jesus' blood,
And the Lord has pardoned all my sins.

14 The road is all ablaze with light
And the gates stand open wide.
The light-house on the river's bank I see,
The angels are a watching me as I approach the shore.
I am going, yes, I'm going over there.

15 I shall wear a starry crown in that land;
In that land, that happy land;
I shall wear a starry crown in that land,
In that happy land.

16 We have an anchor that keeps the soul,
Steadfast and sure while the billows roll;
Fastened to the rock that cannot move,
Grounded firm and deep in the Saviour's love.

17 Full Salvation, full and free,
I have got it and it just suits me;
I plunged into the crimson flood,
The blood of Jesus cleanses me as white as snow.

18 All the way to Calvary He went for me,
He went for me, He went for me;
All the way to Calvary He went for me,
And now He sets me free.

19 Pass along the watch-word, shout it as you go,
Victory, yes victory, over every foe.

20 Happy day, happy day, happy day, happy day,
When Jesus, my Saviour, my sins washed away.

21 I drink when I'm dry, I drink a supply,
I drink from the fountain that never runs dry.

22 It's no harm to know that I love Jesus,
It's no harm to know that I love the Lord.

23 You are drifting to your doom,
You are drifting to your doom,
You are drifting to your doom,
You are drifting to your doom.
Yet there's mercy still for you,
Yet there's mercy still for you,
Yet there's mercy still for you,
Yet there's mercy still for you.

24 I'm going to see my Jesus in the morning,
And I mean to go to heaven bye and bye:
Oh, I'm going to see my Jesus in the morning,
Sinner, don't you want to go to heaven when you die?

25
Peace, peace, wonderful peace,
Joy, joy, none can destroy
Love, love, so boundless and free,
All this my Lord gives to me.

26
Stay on the rock, stay on the rock,
Stay on the rock a little longer, children.
Stay on the rock, stay on the rock,
Stay on the rock a little longer.

27
I'm so glad, I'm so glad
I'm so glad that Jesus saves
And grace is free,
I'm so glad, I'm so glad
I'm so glad that Jesus came,
And He come to save me.

28
|| : I can, I will, I do believe, : ||
That Jesus saves me now.
Just now by faith I do believe
That Jesus saves me now,
He writes the pardon on my heart
As soon as I believe.

154

Jesus Gave Me Rest.

1 Once I was wretched with doubts and fears,
Oft would my pillow be bathed in tears.
But when I trusted, in spite of fears,
Jesus gave me rest.

CHORUS.

Jesus gave me rest, Jesus gave me rest,
Just when I trusted His power to save,
Jesus gave me rest.

2 Long have I striven from sin to flee,
Wishing my Saviour would set me free;
When I was willing to trust, not see;
Jesus gave me rest.

3 I am so happy from day to day,
Often my path is a thorny way;
But close to my Saviour's side I stay.
Jesus gave me rest.

4 Glory to Jesus my song shall be,
Now, and all through eternity,
When I was longing to be set free,
Jesus gave me rest.

5 You, who are tired of doubts and fears,
You, who have wept o'er your sins for years,
Come to the Saviour who dried my tears,
He will give you rest.

INDEX.

MANUFACTURED BY F. H. GILSON CO., BOSTON, MASS.